A Step-by-Step Guide to Genealogy on the World Wide Web

SEARCHING FOR CYBER-ROOTS

BY LAURIE AND STEVE BONNER

D1557806

Ancestry®

http://www.ancestry.com

Bonner, Laurie, 1964–
Searching for cyber-roots : a step-by-step guide to genealogy on the
World Wide Web / by Laurie and Steve Bonner.
    p.   cm.
Includes bibliographical references and index.
ISBN 0-916489-78-7 (softcover)
1. Genealogy—Computer network resources.
2. Web sites—Directories. I. Bonner, Steve, 1959– . II. Title.
CS21.B73   1997
025.06'9291'072—dc21   97-15558

© 1997 Laurie and Steve Bonner
Published by Ancestry Incorporated
P.O. Box 476
Salt Lake City, Utah 84110-0476

First printing 1997
10 9 8 7 6 5 3 2 1

Printed in the United States of America

Contents

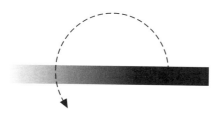

Preface

I T'S BEEN A HECK OF A CENTURY, HASN'T IT?

Only a lifetime ago, a horse and buggy were all you needed to get to the railroad depot or the steamship pier; from there you could travel the world!

Then we learned to zip around so quickly in our cars and our jets—and even our space shuttle—that we began to forget how large the world really is. And with our latest new vehicle, the personal computer, the world is growing yet another step smaller.

Computers do one thing that makes them a boon to genealogists (and, indeed, to nearly everyone else in the modern world!): They store and retrieve data faster and more efficiently than any human ever could. Recent personal computers can store a few gigabytes of data (that's billions of characters). That's enough memory to store the entire *Encyclopaedia Britannica*. With two computers, you could store that and the entire, unabridged *Oxford English Dictionary*. Now imagine that you have the storage and retrieval capacity of 5 million computers—most of them much larger and more powerful than yours—at your fingertips. It boggles the mind, doesn't it?

Well, you do have that power. It's called the Internet. And it's probably the best thing to happen to genealogical research since the invention of the index card. The Internet is a little like the "improbability drive" of the science fiction humorist Douglas Adams. This imaginary form of propulsion allows intrepid space travelers to be everywhere in the universe, all at the same time. So, too, with the Internet! Just click a button and you can be in Sweden. With another click, you're in Singapore. You can consult census data that was recorded a hundred years ago in a sleepy little town an ocean away. And you don't need a spaceship, or even a jet. Just point and click. All over the world, genealogists are coming together via this new communications medium and sharing their knowledge. They're building a new community, and you're invited to join it.

Cyber-Roots will help you get there. Even if you've never touched a personal computer before, this book will give you the chance to start at the very beginning, to learn what kind of a computer you need to buy and what it means to be "online." You'll learn about the different routes you can take to get to the Internet and what kinds of tools and resources will be ready and waiting for you once you get there.

If you don't need to start at the very beginning, skip ahead to the more advanced chapters, where you'll learn more about how the Internet can revolutionize your genealogical research. You'll learn many ways to connect with your peers and to access large genealogical databases available only online. Along the way you'll find powerful new software tools and methods of preserving and presenting your genealogy that would shock your ancestors. (Imagine explaining to your great-grandparents that their wedding portrait has been digitized and distributed to the world! Where would you begin?) Finally, you'll find easy, step-by-step instructions for placing the results of your research where millions of people the world over can share it.

The Internet isn't replacing the days spent rooting through the files in a dusty corner of a small-town courthouse, or wading through high grass to run fingers over a faded tombstone, or squinting at microfiche amidst the hum of a big library. But it will add a new dimension to your journey, and soon the flicker of a computer screen will become as familiar to you as your notebooks, file folders, and index cards. Whether your goal is to publish on the World Wide Web, or just to get to know it a little better, this book will help guide your steps. Enjoy the trip.

CHAPTER 1

A Brief History of the Internet

Y OU SELDOM PICK UP A MAGAZINE OR NEWSPAPER ANYMORE WITHOUT SEEING SOMETHING ABOUT THE INTERNET. And while all the hype may seem overblown, the Internet really is a tremendous communication tool, and it holds great potential for genealogical research.

Even if you've never touched a personal computer before, don't worry. It's never too late to catch up. This chapter will start at the very beginning to tell you exactly what you need to know to get up and running on the information superhighway.

You'll learn:

- *What the Internet is*
- *A little history*
- *Some short answers to the "great unanswerable questions"*
- *What you need to go online*

What Is the Internet, Anyway?

Imagine trying to explain the telephone to George Washington. You could start with a definition—"it's a way to transmit your voice over long distances." You could explain that the entire world is crisscrossed with a vast communications network that enables people on different continents to talk to each other as if they were in the same room. On a simpler level, you could explain that you pick up this "thing," you punch some buttons, and you can talk to someone else in another state. No matter which approach you choose, you're likely to find yourself facing a wrinkled brow and a confused, disbelieving stare.

The Internet is also very hard to describe to someone who's never used it. It's a completely new thing, and it just doesn't fit in with any existing frames of reference. The Internet is a communications network, like the phone system. It includes published material, like newspapers and magazines. It offers video and sound "bites," like cable television. But the Internet is not exactly like any of those things. And the simplest definition, that it's a "network of networks," doesn't tell the whole story either.

Probably the best way to begin to grasp both the complexity and the simplicity of the Internet is to understand how it was born. No one person, place, or entity "created" the Internet. Instead, today's Internet evolved slowly over nearly thirty years.

ARE YOU READY
FOR THE REVOLUTION?

I s this really the Information Revolution or is all such talk just overblown hype? Maybe. Or maybe not. It's too soon to tell for sure, but there are some striking parallels between the developments of the Industrial Revolution and life in the late twentieth century.

Before the Industrial Revolution, which began in England in the mid-1700s, most people lived in small villages and subsistence farms; even the great cities were tiny by modern standards. Travel was limited to horse—and ox—power, and economies were localized. Without good, reliable roads, a crop failure in one locality meant hunger, even if neighboring counties had plenty.

Then, new technologies, such as the steam engine and various new manufacturing tools, created new opportunities. More people came into cities to work in the new factories. More efficient production created a demand for more raw materials, which caused more land to be cleared for larger and more efficient farms. Better trans-

A Little History

Most people remember 1969 as the year an astronaut first stepped on the Moon, but another event occurred in 1969 that may have an even greater effect on the way we will all live our lives tomorrow. On September 1, 1969, researchers at UCLA, Stanford Research Institute, the University of Utah, and the University of California at Santa Barbara succeeded in sending data from computer to computer over telephone lines. Technologically, this was a big step because computers handle data differently than telephones do; the data had to be "translated" into a form the telephone lines would accept and then "re-translated" at the other end. The modem, a computer's version of a telephone handset, fulfills this function today.

This original computer network was dubbed the ARPAnet, after the U.S. Advanced Research Project Agency, which funded the research. The ARPAnet's goal was to help scientists in differ-

--➤

portation systems had to be built to bring raw materials into the cities and to put manufactured products on the market.

By the early 1800s, much of the population was centered in large cities. Fewer people were working larger farms. Developing nations were laced with reliable roads, as well as canals and railroads. This new surplus of goods helped to build national economies capable of steady international trade. And a new middle class was buying Wedgewood, dining with fine crystal and china, and enjoying a life quite different than their agrarian grandfathers had led.

And now? Personal computers

and advanced networking technology are again changing the way people work. In a few short years, computers became integral to our lives. Could you imagine using a bank today that relied on paper ledger sheets to track your accounts? Would you do your taxes without a calculator? Would you fly on an airline that used only a windsock to check the weather and the pilot's eyes to navigate?

Many of the conditions that created the world of the post-Industrial Revolution are beginning to reverse themselves. While factories forced many people to congregate in cities, computers allow people to work from home, wherever home may be—across town or across the globe. Already, U.S. companies are hiring programmers who work in Korea and Taiwan to create software for U.S.-based systems. Their work travels through high-speed communication lines.

While roads, railroads, and airlines are vital to moving manufactured goods, advanced telecommunications may dramatically decrease the demand for travel. Why fly to the next city when you could attend your meetings by teleconference? And while the Internet can't duplicate the experience of standing in the Louvre, you can visit places like WebMuseum, Paris (http://www.oir.ucf.edu/wm.oaint/auth/)

and view dozens of masterpieces much more often than you could probably afford to fly to France.

And while national economies grew around tariffs and duties, individual consumers can now purchase goods directly from overseas—without paying import taxes. The Internet Bookshop (http://www. bookshop.co.uk), for example, is based in England; purchasing books from it via the Internet is much cheaper than buying imported books from booksellers in America.

In the coming decades, perhaps people will travel less. Populations may return to the smaller towns of

---→

ent locations work together on shared research. Over the next few years, more and more universities connected their computers to the ARPAnet.

In 1972, the ARPAnet was displayed at an international conference for computer scientists and researchers. Thrilled by the new capabilities it offered, researchers took this new knowledge home and began building their own versions of the ARPAnet all over the world.

In 1975, the Defense Communications Agency of the U.S. Department of Defense took control of the ARPAnet for its Defense Data Network program. The Department of Defense was attracted to the ARPAnet because it was an "uninterruptible" communications tool. When you make a phone call, your signal bounces through a series of switching networks that send out "feelers" to the many potential paths your signal could take and seek the fastest, most efficient route. Likewise, if any part of the ARPAnet were disrupted, say by enemy bombs, the Department of Defense would still be able to keep its command centers, missile silos, and satellite receivers in touch with each other. In 1983, the Department of Defense decided that it probably wasn't a good

their roots, and "economically disadvantaged" areas may become a thing of the past if electronic commerce continues to erase geographic distances. We may also witness the dawn of a truly global economy as people begin to routinely purchase goods and services from all over the globe. And for a minimal cost, anyone can hang out a shingle and peddle goods and services around the world. The giant supercorporations that grew out of the Industrial Revolution may give way to legions of self-sufficient, independent entrepreneurs who are quite capable of making a comfortable living from their homes.

These conclusions may be speculative, but given the changes that are already occurring, they are not outlandish. In England, the sweeping social and demographic changes of the Industrial Revolution took place in about fifty years. We've had personal computers for less than twenty years, and the Internet has become a tool for the general public within only the last five years. As telecommunications technology grows and improves in the coming decades, and as a new generation comes of age in a world dominated by electronic technology, perhaps the world will sweep through a new cycle of change.

idea to have sensitive military communications traveling on the same highway everyone else uses, so it broke off and created its own separate network.

Also in 1983, technology took another step forward when the networking standards protocol, the "language" computers use when they share information with other computers, was upgraded to something called TCP/IP (Transfer Control Protocol/Internet Protocol). The average user doesn't need to know what these terms mean on a technical level, but the important point is to understand the impact of this protocol. All of the computers in the ARPAnet were quite similar; while sharing information between them took some translation, there were still many computers in the world that couldn't speak their language.

In addition to its strong unifying effect, the combination of TCP and IP provided greater reliability than some other protocols. When paired, TCP and IP guarantee that your messages or files will reach their destination. Even if small portions ("packets") must be retransmitted, all of the pieces will be reassembled at their destination. Furthermore, the Internet Protocol provided greater flexibility in that it allowed information to take any of a number of routes between sender and receiver, passing through intermediate "nodes" of the network. This put some "smarts" into the network itself, without requiring that the human beings at either end know the exact path their communication would follow. As it would later turn out, this was a valuable feature to have when many millions of people would try to talk to one another—many of them all at once!

Meanwhile, the ARPAnet wasn't the only show in town. Several other groups that had been unwilling or unable to speak the networking languages of the ARPAnet had been building their own networks. And those other networks around the world were still growing, too. Imagine a globe covered with starfish whose arms never actually touch each other; each individual computer network spread its arms out to machines within its own domain, but they didn't overlap each other, and you couldn't access one network from the other. An individual user couldn't go any further than the end of a starfish's arm.

When the ARPAnet led the way toward adopting TCP/IP,

BULLETIN BOARD SYSTEMS: TO EACH ACCORDING TO HIS PROTOCOL

During the 1980s, while the Internet was forming, another movement was attempting to accomplish much the same thing. In local communities computer enthusiasts transmitted e-mail and files between computers using Bulletin Board Systems (BBSs). BBS screens in the 1980s were character-based (no interesting graphics), and screen updates were made at the painfully slow transfer rates of that era, such as 1200 or 2400 baud (a baud is roughly equivalent to a bit [a binary digit—the fundamental unit of information processed by computers] per second). Users would select options from a menu that allowed them to send mail to other users of the BBS, or to upload or download files. They could enter "rooms" that would allow them to play character-based games. Each BBS was operated by its own

suddenly it became possible to communicate with other networks. Throughout the 1980s, the people who controlled all of these separate, independent networks began building bridges, called "gateways," to interconnect their systems. Imagine that those starfish on the globe all move their arms so that they overlap, end-to-end. Now, a user could sit down at a computer and travel from one network to another—as far as the connections could reach. These people were creating one giant "interconnected network"; hence the term "Internet."

This giant network was poised for unprecedented growth. Many people consider January 1, 1983, the date the ARPAnet adopted TCP/IP, to be the true birth date of the Internet.

Through the 1980s, many more people brought new systems and networks into the Internet, and soon traffic jams were developing. This situation was something like the roads in the United States in the middle of the twentieth century. If you wanted to drive from, say, Miami to Boston, you had to drive the whole distance on two-lane roads, stopping at every stop light in the heart of every town

----

SYStem OPerator (SYSOP), who controlled all aspects of the BBS.

There was—and still is—a wide variety of BBS software and hardware products that allow even a not-very-powerful personal computer to host a BBS. Originally, transferring data to or from a BBS required that the machines on both ends be running the same type of software. File transfer methods had names like X-MODEM, Y-MODEM, Z-MODEM. If your computer didn't speak the exact "dialect" used by the host machine, you weren't able to communicate. Because of these differences, BBSs couldn't always talk to one another.

As the Internet continued to grow, BBS users found that they wanted to communicate with people on the Internet or with people on other BBSs. Some BBSs were connected to the Internet through gateways—computers that understand more than one protocol and are able to act as translators; this increased the flexibility of BBSs, but they have to a large extent been overtaken by events. Although BBSs are still in existence, the vast majority of travelers in "cyberspace" today are connected to the Internet through an Internet service provider or a commercial online service. (See chapter 2.)

along the way. Likewise, if a 1985 Internet user at the University of Miami wanted to contact a colleague at Harvard, the signal was routed through every local system and network, on low-speed lines, along the way. But user traffic was growing, and rush-hour-like bottlenecks were slowing down the network.

In 1987, the National Science Foundation set out on a program to increase the use of supercomputers, and one of its projects included NSFnet, a high-speed supercomputer "backbone" for Internet traffic.

Now, if you want to drive your car from Miami to Boston, you drive out of Miami and get onto Interstate 95, which carries you on a fast, direct, non-stop trip to the Boston area, where you get off and find your local destination. Likewise, the NSFnet picks up the Miami user's Internet transmission and carries it quickly and directly to the Boston area, where it drops off into a local network and seeks its local address.

Comparing NSFnet to I-95 is a bit simplistic; just as many other highways and secondary roads intersect or run parallel to I-95, so there are many layers in the NSFnet. But the NSFnet brought several important innovations: in addition to carrying users non-stop past series of local networks, the NSFnet also "widened the road" so that computer traffic could move in bigger "chunks." That ability to carry more traffic, at higher speeds, in larger volumes gave users a new option: graphics.

Before the NSFnet, all Internet traffic was text-based; people communicated by typing long, arcane strings of code, and all of the information that was stored and retrieved consisted of simple letters and numbers. And the only people who were using the Net were the scientists, researchers, and students who were willing to spend many hours learning how to use it.

But several factors that would open the Net to more popular use converged in the late 1980s. Mouse-driven point-and-click interfaces, introduced on the early Apple personal computers and later on the Microsoft Windows operating system, were becoming standard on all types of machines. Because such interfaces made using computers easier, the use of personal computers was exploding in the workplace, and more people were becoming familiar with basic operations of Windows and Apple Macintoshes. And the graphics capability introduced by NSFnet engendered the birth of the World Wide Web.

Remember DOS? At one time, in the 1980s, all IBM computers ran on DOS, or the Disk Operating System, which was the underlying software that allowed the computer to run other software. All you saw when you turned on your computer was a prompt (a:/>), and you had to type in all your commands. The first versions of Microsoft Windows were just easier-to-learn point-and-click

WHO'S OUT THERE?

No one can ever be entirely sure how many people are connected to the Internet. It's like counting fish in a crowded aquarium; by the time you get close, they've all moved around and you can't be sure whom you've already counted. People open and close Internet accounts every day. Some people have more than one account, and sometimes several people share a single account.

Nevertheless, The Panos Institute, an international nonprofit research organization specializing in development issues, has published a report that estimates Internet usage around the world. It reveals some chilling possibilities for nations that are unable to "plug in."

According to Panos, more than 40 million people in one hundred countries have direct access to the Internet. An additional fifty-eight nations have limited e-mail access. In September 1995, the Internet comprised 6.7 million documents stored on 5 million "host" computers, 70 percent of which are located in the United States; since then, that quantity of documents has grown at a rate of about 1 percent per day. By May 1996, the search engine AltaVista reported that it had indexed 30 million documents, and by October 1996, another engine, HotBot, reported 54 million documents. Keep in mind that any one search engine (software that allows a user to search documents on the Web for specified keywords; see chapter 3 for more information) indexes only a fraction of the total documents on the World Wide Web, and that the Web in turn contains only a fraction of what is available on the entire Internet!

It's a brave new world but, unfortunately, one that is also creating a *new form of illiteracy. Access to the Internet requires a phone line, but forty-nine nations (thirty-five of which are in Africa) have fewer than one telephone per one hundred people. According to Panos, there are more phone lines on Manhattan Island in New York than in the whole of sub-Saharan Africa, and half of the world's population has never made a phone call.*

Cost is also an issue. For a person of the Western working class, a new computer system may be the equivalent of several paychecks. In

Indonesia, a working class person would have to pay several years' income for the same computer. And even in sectors of the world that have built telecommunications networks, the cost of using the phone for a month can exceed the cost of more basic needs, like food.

For a more in-depth discussion of these issues and others that will affect how the Internet will change the world, read the Panos report at: http://www.oneworld.org/panos/panos_internet_press.html

---

interfaces that made it easier to interact with DOS.

The World Wide Web (or simply "the Web") is a point-and-click interface that allows people to interact with the Internet without having to type in long commands. And, just as Windows introduced new graphics capabilities that DOS couldn't handle as well, so has the Web introduced new capabilities to the Internet. And it's the Web that handles the pictures, sound, and video that are making the Internet more exciting and more accessible to more and more people every day.

The World Wide Web was invented by Tim Berners-Lee in 1990 while he was working at the European Laboratory for Particle Physics (CERN) in Switzerland. It was originally designed to allow scientists to communicate information uniformly and easily by allowing them to jump smoothly between documents or portions of documents. The Web also provided a mechanism for integrating graphics and other types of data. By encapsulating a document with a standard header and other "markup tags" written in the HyperText Markup Language (HTML), Berners-Lee laid the foundation for the Web that we know today.

The World Wide Web is not synonymous with the Internet. The Web is the part of the Internet's traffic that encompasses graphics and point-and-click interfaces. Many uses of the Internet, such as e-mail, file transfers, and other text-based communications, do not involve the Web.

In 1993, when President Clinton delivered his first State of the Union address, one of the goals he cited was the building of the national "information infrastructure," now also called the "information superhighway." That's when the nation's reporters and editors scratched their heads and said, "The what?" And that's when major cover stories began appearing in national publications such as *Time* and *Newsweek* heralding the wonders of the Internet and the World Wide Web.

The project, known on Capitol Hill as the High Performance Computer Act, had originally been proposed by then-Senator Albert Gore, who brought it into the presidential limelight. Its goal is to build the National Research and Education Network (NREN), a nationwide network of better, stronger, and faster supercomputers. Currently many Americans, especially those who live in rural areas, are limited to phone systems with decades-old copper wiring that is not capable of handling state-of-the-art electronic traffic. Just as the Interstate Highways Act of the 1950s built highways to the far reaches of rural America, NREN will carry high-speed trafficking capabilities to all corners of the nation.

Notice that the terms "information superhighway" and "Internet" are also not synonymous. Information superhighway refers to the system of powerful computers that is capable of handling high volumes of fast-networking traffic. The Internet is the traffic, or communication, that travels on that highway. There are also some questions still about who will be able to use NREN; because it's a government project, the funding must be allocated to government agencies, and NREN's stated purpose is to handle traffic strictly for government and university use. The Internet was once a government and university tool, but it now handles a wide variety of traffic for individuals, commercial interests, professional associations, charities, organizations, and anyone else you can imagine. When it is built, NREN may not allow public traffic. Many users believe, though, that since the Internet has so thoroughly pervaded American life, public traffic will make it onto whatever structure becomes available.

The Great "Unanswerable" Questions

So what is the Internet? Who owns it? Who pays for it? Who governs it? This quick historical overview should give you a new perspective on these questions:

What is it? The Internet today is a vast network of networks, linking millions of computers all over the planet. All of the information that is available on the Internet was put there specifically so that you can use it. And the Internet has unique characteristics that set it apart from every other communications tool that has ever existed. It's interactive; you decide what you want to see or hear, and you can communicate directly with the person who provided that information. It's uninterruptible; Internet traffic flows through millions of computers around the globe. Even if one or more component computers "crashes," or goes offline, no single interruption can bring down the entire Internet. (See "Who's Out There?," page 9.) To stop the information flow, you'd have to destroy all of them at once. It's interconnected seamlessly; you can access information from Australia just as easily as you can access your neighborhood library. And you may not even know where you're going. A single click of the mouse may take you to Sweden; your next click could take you to India or Senegal.

You don't need to learn a dozen languages to use the Internet, either. Because the Internet was born and grew up in the United States, the dominant language is English, even for material that originates in non-English-speaking nations. That dominance may change, however, as French, Spanish, German, Dutch, Japanese, and other languages begin to appear.

Who owns it? Everyone. And no one. No single person or entity "owns" the Internet. All of those pieces of the network that have been connected all over the world were created by individuals who wanted to build a part of the Internet; each person is responsible for maintaining his or her own piece of the whole, and each person "owns" only that piece. So the Internet is co-owned by all of its millions of contributors.

🌀 **Who pays for it?** Everyone. And no one. Each person who has built a piece of the network bears the cost of maintaining his or her own piece. A common myth is that the Internet is "free." That's true in the sense that no one is officially in charge of selling access to the Internet as a whole. But many different people own pieces of the Net that act like entrance ramps, and you have to pay a toll to use their ramps. Also, many people who work for the universities and government institutions that created the Internet have "free" access, but that's only because it's their employers who are paying.

🌀 **Who governs it?** Once more: Everyone. And no one. The Internet has no president or CEO. But there is an organization called the Internet Society, which acts more like a congress than a president. The ISOC sets standards on the technical elements that keep all those disparate computers talking to each other. It also creates structured naming conventions so that, for example, all e-mail addresses look the same, just as all telephone numbers in the United States have the same number of digits and use the same structure: area code, exchange, and personal extension. (See chapter 3.) The ISOC is a voluntary membership organization, and all of its work is done by volunteers in committees.

Recently the U.S. Congress and some other national governments have passed laws that have attempted to place jurisdiction on the Internet, mostly concerning issues of censorship and pornography. But most people in the Internet community have scoffed at the efforts, and it takes only a rudimentary understanding of the Net to see why. Because the Internet crosses international borders so easily, no one government can possibly regulate it. If the U.S. Congress outlaws pornography on the Net, anyone in America can still access the material from computers all over the world—say, in Belgium or Japan—where U.S. laws don't apply. And nothing's going to stop an American from posting pornography on a computer in Toronto.

But the Internet is raising complex liability issues, and many governments around the world are scrutinizing ways to keep unwanted material away from their borders. Can Germany require CompuServe to block access to pornographic material from users all over the world—just to shield German citizens? Can China fine, or even arrest, an American in San Francisco for posting inflammatory statements on a computer in Beijing? In the years to come, you can expect to see some interesting issues debated in courts around the world.

Because the Net is so complex, with so many computers wired into it, any one signal could travel through millions of different routes. So it's also impossible to build "roadblocks"; any barrier could be circumvented. If you're a parent who has hesitated to bring the Internet into your home for fear of exposing your child to some of the roughness of the adult world, the only reliable way to control access to the highway is right in your own driveway. Many commercial products are available that are easy to use and will help you control your child's use of the Net.

If all of this information seems overwhelming, don't worry about it. You don't need a degree in civil engineering to drive safely across the Golden Gate Bridge. And when you pick up the phone and dial New Zealand, you don't need to worry about how your signal is bouncing through a series of local transmitters, switching stations, and even a satellite or two. All that matters to you is that someone on the other end picks up the receiver and says "Hello."

Likewise, you don't really need to worry about how many computers and high-speed data lines are carrying the Internet. All you need to know is that you can sit down at your home computer and access an incredible amount of information from other computers all over the world.

What Do You Need to Go Online?

The two most basic tools for going online are a computer and a modem. You don't need to sink tens of thousands of dollars into a souped-up Porsche of a home computer to use the Internet, but you should purchase the most powerful computer you can afford because, on the Internet, time is money. The faster your computer can process graphics and the faster your modem moves information, the sooner you'll log off. You can use the Internet with a slower computer, but the response times will be so very slow that you'll quickly become frustrated, and your connection charges could overwhelm your budget.

Any of the basic systems on the market today, such as the Pentiums or the PowerMacs, will give you a perfectly adequate Internet connection. You can buy some slower but acceptable machines for as little as $1,500, but expect to pay something in the range of $2,000 for a system that will keep you going for a few years.

If you are considering buying a used machine, or if you want to assess whether your two- or three-year-old computer will handle the job, make sure you meet the following standards. These numbers represent the absolute *minimum* you should buy for a comfortable ride on the Net:

🌀 **100 MHZ.** MHZ, or megahertz, refers to how many times the computer's "brain," or microprocessor, "thinks" in a second. The higher the number, the more calculations per second it can perform, and the faster a response to your command will appear on your screen. Many new computers run at well over 200 MHZ.

🌀 **1 Gigabyte Hard Disk.** One gigabyte is equal to approximately 1 billion characters' worth of information. While the size of your hard disk won't directly affect the speed of your Internet connection, if it's not large enough, you won't be able to retrieve and store as much data without interfering with the number of programs you can run.

32 MB RAM. Megabytes (MB) of random access memory (RAM) refers to how much information your computer can "juggle" at once while it operates. Higher RAM numbers mean you can run more complex programs. Many computers will allow you to "upgrade," or add more RAM.

28.8 or 33.6 kbps Modem. The modem is your computer's telephone— its link to the outside world. The number refers to the speed with which the modem can send and receive data, which is measured in kilobits per second (kbps). A 33.6 kbps modem is faster than a 28.8 kbps modem, which in turn is noticeably faster than a 14.4 kbps modem—and time is money when you're paying for Web connection by the hour. If you already own a 14.4 kbps modem, you can get by with what you have for now, especially if your principal use of the Internet is for e-mail. But to do any serious Web-surfing, you'll need a faster modem.

If you're shopping for a new modem, you'll face another choice: You can buy an internal modem, which is a card that is installed inside your computer, or an external one, which is a separate "box" about the size of a paperback book that sits beside your computer. Each type has its advantages and drawbacks.

The *internal* modem is cheaper. It doesn't add an extra piece of clutter to your desk, and you don't have to turn the power on and off each time you use it. But you do have to open up your computer to install it.

The *external* modem is out where you can see it, and it has a row of lights on the front that show you when it's working. That may seem like a minor point, but when you're waiting for a connection on the Internet, and nothing seems to be happening on the screen, you can tell at a glance, if the modem's lights are flickering, that your modem is chugging along and you just need to be patient. Plus, with only a few cords to plug in, it's easier to install.

These are the most basic numbers you need to get online. But

DO I REALLY
NEED A COMPUTER?

The answer to that question is a tentative "No."

In late 1996, WebTV made its debut, heralded by holiday advertising proclaiming that now you can surf the Web from your television.

When you buy a WebTV unit, you're essentially buying a stripped-down personal computer; the WebTV unit becomes the "computer," your television becomes the monitor, and it connects into a standard phone jack at 33.6 kbps. With a remote control and an optional wireless keyboard, you're ready to go.

WebTV is simple to use; all of its software is preloaded, and service with an Internet "service provider" is prearranged. And at about $350, WebTV is far cheaper than the four-figure prices for personal computers.

So what's the problem?

WebTV will allow you to send and receive e-mail as well as display information on any Web site. But WebTV has no disk drives, so it won't let you upload or download files of data or software. And there's no way to connect a printer, so you can't print out copies of the data you find. To a genealogist, those omissions could be critical.

Still, if you absolutely don't want or can't afford a computer, WebTV offers you a viable alternative.

you'll also face some other choices:

CD-ROM Drive. For years now software houses have distributed products that are available only on CD-ROM, and many of the newer multimedia products require a drive that operates at a particular speed. A CD-ROM drive is not strictly required for using the Internet, but without one you may find that you're missing out on some software packages that you'd really like to use. Many archives and companies have published censuses, courthouse records, and other genealogical source data on CD-ROM.

SVGA Monitor. Most new computers come with higher resolution Super VGA monitors, which display clearer graphics with more colors than older VGA monitors. (VGA stands for video graphics array; it's been standard equipment on personal computers for more than a decade. Unless you have a very old computer, it's unlikely that your monitor will not support VGA or comparable graphics.) Some of the more advanced graphics and animations on the Web will display well only on SVGA monitors. But if you already have a VGA monitor, it will be more than adequate to display most of what you'll find.

Sound Cards and Speakers. Like a CD-ROM drive, the capability to hear sound is not mandatory for the average person who is surfing the Net. While you'll need a sound card (a piece of hardware installed inside your computer) in order to hear any music or sound effects that are accessible on the Internet, "soundbites" are still a very minor part of the Net, and they aren't necessary for genealogical research. Perhaps someday it will be more common for people to incorporate soundbites—recordings of their grandparents' reminiscences, for example—into their genealogical records. However, many of the CD-ROMs available today, especially state-of-the-art games, require sound cards.

Many people hesitate to buy home computers because the technology changes so quickly that they seem to be obsolete as soon as they're out of the box. For that reason, you should be cautious about saving a few hundred dollars on a new computer that's already a little behind the times. Many people tell themselves that they'll just buy upgrades in a year or two. While it is possible to buy many pieces separately, such as the CD-ROM drive, sound cards, and RAM cards, installing them is notoriously difficult, and even a professional installation can cause troubles.

On the other hand, as long as your computer is performing as well as you need it to, and running the software you use most frequently, it is not necessary to run out and buy a new computer every time a new feature hits the shelves. If you buy a good, up-to-date computer today, it should last you well into the next century.

CHAPTER 2

Choosing Your On-Ramp

N OW THAT YOU'VE GOT THE RIGHT EQUIPMENT AND YOU'RE PLUGGED IN AND READY TO GO, IT'S TIME TO FIGURE OUT HOW TO REACH THAT ONLINE WORLD.

Just as you need to notify the phone company and set up an account to activate your phone line, you also need to set up an account with someone who will give you Internet access. But, while you usually have only one local phone company and a handful of long distance companies to choose from, you can choose among hundreds of Internet Service Providers (ISPs).

In this chapter, you'll learn:

 *What America Online, CompuServe, and other online services can offer you*

 *How to get online—through an online service or through an ISP*

 *The benefits and drawbacks of each route*

 *How to know which is best for you*

The Commercial Route

The easiest way for a beginner to get online is to use one of the major commercial services, such as CompuServe, America Online, or the Microsoft Network. These names are not synonymous with the Internet. In chapter 1 we defined the Internet as a vast network of unique networks that communicate with each other through gateways. America Online is just one network that connects to the Internet-at-large; CompuServe and the Microsoft Network do the same.

All will allow you to send e-mail to anyone, anywhere on the Internet. All will allow you to go out and browse on the World Wide Web and to seek and retrieve documents and access other services from around the world. However, each one maintains features and services that are available only within its own network to its own members.

If you join American Online, for example, you can interact in live chat rooms with other America Online members, you can use America Online's exclusive services, and you can cross onto the Internet. But you cannot view CompuServe screens or access CompuServe's exclusive services.

Genealogy on the Commercial Services

Both America Online and CompuServe have areas devoted to genealogy ("Genealogy Forum" and "Roots Forum," respectively) that are designed to help you find and communicate with other genealogists. Each service's area is available only to members of that commercial service.

Start by reading "Frequently Asked Questions" and other features for new members. You'll find specific, step-by-step instructions for getting around and accessing the different parts of the area. With any commercial service you have three fundamental ways to communicate:

🌀 **Conference rooms** let you engage in live "chat" sessions with other members of your service. Chat areas work like normal conversations, except that you type in your comments at the bottom of your screen. As soon as you click on "SEND," your message appears on a "public" area in the middle of your screen. Anyone else in your "chat room" will read your note, and someone else can type a response, which will instantly appear in the public area for you to read. The effect is like having an actual conversation with several people, except that those people may be scattered from Alaska to Maine to Florida.

While you probably won't find much fodder for your genealogy research in the general chat rooms, both of the commercial services offer chat sessions specifically for people who want to discuss genealogy. A schedule of events is posted in the services' genealogy areas, so you can know when to "meet" with special interest groups for people doing research in many regional and ethnic categories. While it's unlikely (but not impossible!) that you'll encounter someone researching the same ancestors you are, you will find people who've tackled the same problems you have. And someone might tell you about a small historical library you didn't know existed, how to read "old-style" Quaker dates, or where to find slave records for a particular plantation in Georgia.

Message boards are another way to reach people if you're not finding the answers you need in the chat rooms. These work sort of like classified ads; you post a note with a question about a line you're researching, and you check back a few days later to see if someone has posted a reply. While you can post all types of general and specific questions, the message boards are more likely to provide you with answers to very specific questions about your ancestors than are the chat rooms. What was this woman's maiden name, and who were her parents? When did this family immigrate? Where did this man come from before suddenly showing up in Wyoming?

Message boards don't offer the instant communication that you'll find in the chat rooms, but these messages stay posted for months, so, if you have specific questions, the chances are pretty good that eventually someone will have an answer for you. If you like, you can include your e-mail address in your message, and someone may contact you directly.

You can also browse through the messages that have already been posted. They are easy to search and are organized by surname, state, and nationality. Other message boards address general genealogy questions and computer tools for genealogists.

🌀 **Libraries** offer a set of common genealogy software and other materials you can copy to your own machine for your personal use. You'll find GEDCOM database files (used to transfer genealogical data between otherwise incompatible software packages or computers), tiny tafels (a compact text format in which the contents of a family database can be summarized and readily provided to other researchers), graphics support files to let you handle photographs and maps, and a variety of other offerings for DOS, Macintosh, and Windows environments. You may also find archives of messages from the message boards and references to various books and publications. While you may not be able to access the books directly online, you may find leads to material you didn't know existed.

The online services offer related subjects that also interest genealogists. For example, research areas use all three of these types of online communications to help people specifically with research methods, and America Online features a history area designed to help you learn more about the historical context of the ancestors you're researching. The history area is organized by region, ethnic group, and time period, and it includes message boards and chat areas pertaining to these topics. But the emphasis here is more on events than on specific people. You'll find lots of information on the U.S. Civil War and various periods of U.S. immigration.

The ISP Route

The commercial services offer you gateways to the World Wide Web and other parts of the "Internet-at-large." But they also provide additional services, such as chat rooms and special-interest or hobbyist areas, that are available only to members. You can bypass these commercial services and sign on with an ISP that gives you only the Internet access. With this kind of direct hookup to the Internet, you will not have access to the genealogy forums that reside within the commercial services. You will, however, have access to a broad variety of newsgroups, databases, and other genealogical resources located on the Internet itself. These resources are discussed in detail in chapters 4 and 5. While you can access these Internet resources from an online service, you may find that the Internet itself is all you need.

How Do I Get Online?

There are two basic steps to going online: obtaining the software and establishing an account.

If you choose to go the commercial route:

- **Obtaining the software** for the online services is wonderfully easy; they can't wait to give it to you for free, and everything you need is included in one tidy package. If the free disk wasn't included with your new computer, and if you can't find it attached to an ad in a computer magazine, and if you're not among the millions of people on their mailing lists, you can get the software by calling either of these numbers: for America Online, 1-800-827-6364; for CompuServe, 1-800-374-3509; for the Microsoft Network, 1-800-FREE-MSN.

- **Establishing an account** is also fairly simple. After you load the software and the first time you use it to dial out on your modem, you'll go through a series of screens that will prompt you to register. At some point you'll be asked for a credit card number, which the service will use to bill you each month for the time that you spend online. (Here's where a faster modem begins to pay for itself.) Although the exact rates charged by these services are always in flux, you will find that a basic rate can be obtained for under $10 per month. You may pay a slightly higher fixed rate if you want unlimited use. Check the service's web pages for "today's specials!"

If you choose the ISP route:

- **Obtaining the software** is a little more complex. Some ISPs will provide you with the software; others will not. You need to obtain a Web browser, such as Netscape's *Navigator* or

Microsoft's *Internet Explorer,* which enable you to visit sites on the World Wide Web, send e-mail, and read newsgroups. You may want additional software to conduct telnet sessions, transfer files, perform gopher searches, and for other types of access. If your service does not give you the software, you can find a variety of packages, such as *Internet in a Box* or *Internet Valet,* that include everything you need for under $100 in most computer stores. (Here's a catch-22: If you're already online or know someone who is, you can also download much of this software for free. But to be sure you're getting quality products in versions that will function on your machine, it may be safer to buy them.)

Some of the major service providers include NETCOM at 1-800-353-6600, PSI at 1-800-827-7482, and UUNet at 1-800-488-6383. There are dozens of other national providers, as well as hundreds more regional and local providers across the United States. Rates and services vary widely, but you ought to be able to open an account for around $10 per month. Some may offer virtually unlimited hours at no extra charge; others will allow as many as twenty to thirty "free" hours in the base rate. You may also have to pay one-time start-up fees—for example, if you want to register your own domain name.

🌀 **Establishing an account** also takes a little more work. Each major city has a variety of ISPs that sell accounts to individuals. Essentially, you're paying for the right to dial into someone else's computer, which will in turn link you directly to the Internet. To find these providers, look for ads in local publications or ask for help at a local computer store. Rates start at under $10 per month, but quality, rates, and services offered vary widely, so shop around. Be sure to ask:

- How many modem lines does do they support? Too few may mean that you'll constantly get busy signals.

- How fast are their own baud rates? Buying a fast modem of your own won't help you if the machine you're connecting to is slower.

- Will they support the Internet software you've purchased? Not all providers support all of the packages available.

- Do they provide a mail server? In order to send and receive e-mail, your software may require something called Post Office Protocol.

- How much free usage is included in the base rate? You may also have to pay a one-time sign-on charge.

- How do they expect to receive payment? Some want to receive monthly checks; if you're forgetful, you may end up having to constantly restart your service.

Make sure, also, that you've chosen a provider that is within your local calling area; you don't want to pay toll charges in addition to connection charges. Because there are so many providers, quality of customer service varies widely. Some may bend over backwards to answer all of your questions promptly, while some may ignore repeated requests.

Alternate routes may be available in your area. Taking a class or two at a local college may result in the bonus of an Internet account on the school's network. Libraries across the country are offering Internet access to patrons, and some may even allow you to establish a private account for personal e-mail. Many employers also have Internet access and are willing to extend accounts to employees. (But be wary of doing personal research on company time!)

Which Route Should I Take?

There's no one-size-fits-all route to the Internet. It's up to you to try different avenues and find a way that best suits your needs. Here are some benefits and drawbacks to each of your options.

For commercial services:
Benefits:

- It's easy to get up and running with basic Internet access.

- You will find a wealth of help screens, detailed directions, and immediate online technical support from real people to help you with your first steps.

- Each service offers easy access to a variety of shopping, travel, chat, electronic publications, and other services that are available only to its own members.

- The commercial services are working to offer built-in features to make it easier for parents to monitor and control their children's use of the Internet.

- If you travel, you can easily get online almost anywhere with the same account (although the big, national ISPs provide 800 numbers that allow you to do this as well).

Drawbacks:

- If you're not using your provider's exclusive services, you're paying for more than you need.

- If you're not interested in your provider's exclusive services, you have a series of screens to penetrate each time you want to get out to the Internet.

- Any communicating you do in the genealogical research areas will be limited only to other members of that service.

For other ISPs:

Benefits:

- If you're interested only in the Internet-at-large, this is the fastest way to get there.

- Many services—such as publications, travel reservations, stock listings, and shopping—that mimic the commercial services' local offerings are also available on the Internet-at-large.

Drawbacks:

- Finding the software and establishing an account may be more complicated, and you'll find fewer—or no—avenues for online help and support.

- Quality of service varies as widely as the people providing it, so you might have to look harder for a good company. Also, the Internet tends to a volatile place, and these companies can start up and go out of business frequently. You may find yourself switching providers more frequently than you'd like.

- While you'll be able to send e-mail to anyone, you'll have no access to the local features of the commercial providers.

- You'll find a variety of shopping, travel, and other services on the Internet, but you have to seek them yourself. Again, the quality of these services varies according to the skills and integrity of the people who provide them.

- Child-monitoring software is available and easy to use, but you have to buy it separately.

For alternate routes, such as libraries, schools, and employers:

Benefits:

- You can't beat free.

- Someone else has already done the work of choosing software and providers for you.

- Some institutions have much, much faster speeds than are currently available in homes.

Drawbacks:

- You may have to travel to the school's computer lab or to the library or to your office to get online.

- Your access may be limited. If you're using your employer's machines, your e-mail communications will not be private; your boss will have legal access to everything you do.

What it boils down to is this: the commercial services give you everything you need in a quick and easy, quality controlled, prefabricated package. The ISP route is more flexible and powerful, and you can even have all of the services you would want from a commercial provider, but you're on your own to go out and find everything for yourself. The ISP route gives you the freedom to customize your own access to the Internet, but like anything else in life, that freedom also brings added risk and responsibility: it's up to you to find the features you want, to protect your children, and to avoid shoddy services.

You won't know which choices are best for you until you try them. As a beginner, your best bet is to join a commercial service until you've learned your way around. These services offer free trial periods; take advantage of one or more, and see which one offers you the services and environment you want. If you're happy with one of them, keep it. But also spend some time exploring the World Wide Web, the newsgroups, and other Internet features. If you find that you're devoting most of your online time to the Internet itself, and you've found ways to mimic all of the features you'd want from your commercial service, then consider shopping for a separate ISP. Eventually, you'll find the method that works best for you.

IN THE FUTURE

ew options for plugging into the Internet will begin appearing very shortly. Every phone and cable company is jockeying to position itself as your strongest, fastest, and cheapest route. AT&T has begun offering its customers limited free Internet access, and you can bet that MCI and Sprint won't lag far behind.

Over the next three to five years, the rush to offer Internet services will become even more competitive as more

and more people discover the Internet for the first time. Also, as the competition intensifies, watch out as America Online, CompuServe, and the Microsoft Network struggle to offer you more and more reasons to stick with a commercial service.

Who will win? You will. Get online now however you can, but keep an ear to the ground for better ways to get what you want.

CHAPTER 3

Tools of the Trade

OKAY. YOU'RE WIRED UP AND PLUGGED IN, AND YOUR HAND IS POISED ON YOUR MOUSE. NOW WHAT? Whether you've entered through a commercial provider or found your own door, you'll find a wealth of tools and useful information on the Internet. And you are now able to communicate directly with millions of people all over the world. That's an awfully crowded room, especially when you're looking just for the handful of people who are interested in the same research you're doing. So how do you find them?

Today, the World Wide Web offers abundant information for genealogists, but there are other tools you should learn about as well. While the rest of this book will be devoted to using the World Wide Web, in this chapter you'll learn the answers to these questions:

What are the basic Internet tools?

- *Browsers such as* **Netscape Navigator** *or* **Internet Explorer**
- *Search engines*
- *E-mail*
- *Newsreaders*
- *FTP*
- *Telnet*

What do I do with them?

- *Mailing lists*
- *Newsgroups*
- *BBSs*

🌀 What's a Web page?

- *Home pages*
- *Hypertext*
- *HyperText Markup Language*

What Are the Basic Internet Tools?

When most people think of the Internet, they think of the World Wide Web (often called the Web or WWW), which is the portion of the Internet that is capable of handling graphics, sound, video, and hypertext. As we outlined in chapter 1, the Web is a relatively recent addition to the Internet, but it is quickly becoming the most important tool for most users. However, to get the most out of the Internet, you need several different tools:

🌀 **A Web browser,** such as *Internet Explorer* or *Netscape Navigator,* is your tool for interacting with the World Wide Web, just as Windows is the tool that enables you to run your other software.

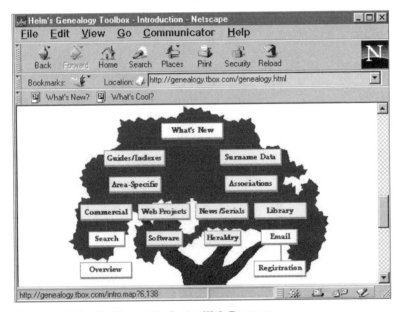

Figure 3-1. The *NetScape Navigator* Web Browser
Copyright 1997 Netscape Communications Corp. All rights reserved. This page may not be reprinted or copied without the express written permission of Netscape. Netscape is a trademark of Netscape Communications Corporation, which is registered in the United States and other countries. Used by permission.

WHAT IS A URL?

A URL, or Uniform Resource Locator, is the unique identifier, or address, that allows your Web browser to locate a document. For example, suppose we had a home page at *http://www.fictitious.com/~tsmith/*. This might look like a string of random letters at first, but there is a pattern.

http://www.fictitious.com/~tsmith/

scheme   domain name   document location

- **The scheme**—*the part preceding the colon (in this case "http")*— *tells you what kind of document you are accessing. HTTP, for HyperText Transfer Protocol, indicates that this document was written in HTML, which is the language used to write documents for the World Wide Web; you can open it and read it with your Web browser. Another common scheme is FTP, for File Transfer Protocol, which indicates a text-based document or maybe a software program that you don't want your browser to try to read; you just want to copy it to your computer so you can read it or use it. Others you might see include FILE for local files, MAILTO for e-mail addresses, and NEWS for newsgroups.*

- **The domain name**—*The part immediately following the colon and the double slash (in our example "www.fictitious.com") indicates the address of the Web server where the document resides. Often, you can read the name of a company or organization in its domain name, such as "www.at&t.com" or "www.pbs.org." The three-letter suffix shows you the type of entity it is, such as ".com" for a company, ".edu" for a college or university, ".gov" for government agencies, or ".org" for a nonprofit or professional organization.*

- **The document location**—*the part following the next slash—takes you to the particular document, or Web page, you want. It may begin with a directory, such as "~tsmith" (the main directory for user or account tsmith). The file name may be explicitly provided, such as "smith_family.html", or, as in our example, may be omitted. When omitted, the default name "index.html" is understood. Of course, a file suffix of ".html" or ".htm" indicates that it is an HTML document written for use with a Web browser.*

If you already know the URL for the page you want, you can type it into the URL text box at the top of your browser's screen. Because it's so easy to mis-type, you should also save the ones you use frequently in "Bookmarks" or "Favorites," which are available from your browser's pull-down menu. (The name varies depending on which browser you're using, but the function is identical.) Then, you'll be able to access that page with an easy point-and-click.

Here's a hint: sometimes when you type in a URL, you will get a message indicating that the file was not found. Try truncating the file name, leaving only the scheme and domain name; sometimes your request will go through, and you will find yourself on the host Web page. From there, you can often proceed to open the document you want.

Your browser is the first thing you see; it's your doorway to the rest of the world. From your browser, you can go to any Web address, or URL, you know. If you don't know the address, but you want to find out if, say, a distant state has a historical society, then you need a search engine.

A search engine, such as WebCrawler, Lycos, AltaVista, or Yahoo!, is an indexing tool that helps you to find interesting

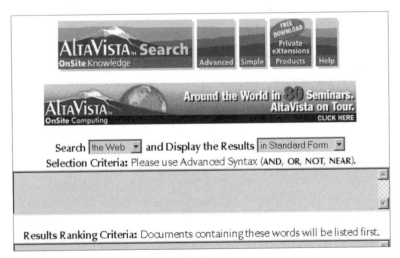

Figure 3-3. The AltaVista Search Engine
Alta Vista is a trademark of Digital Equipment Corporation. Copyright 1997 Digital Equipment Corporation. Used by permission.

places on the Web. These search engines are themselves documents that reside on the Web, and *Internet Explorer* and *Netscape Navigator* both come with built-in links to several. But it's a good idea to add a few more. (See appendix A under "Web Search Engines" for several especially good ones.)

E-mail is one of your most important tools. This is the function that allows you to send notes to anyone else, anywhere on the Internet, as long as you know their e-mail address. In addition to the actual note, you can attach files—graphics, spreadsheets, word processing, GEDCOM, etc.—at no extra cost. The commercial services as well as many TCP/IP software packages allow you to compose mail before you log on as well as download your current mail so that you can read and review it offline. This feature will save you connect charges.

A newsreader is the tool that will take you to Usenet, which is the Internet's network of message boards, called newsgroups. Many genealogists rely on newsgroups to contact other researchers working on the same lines, to share information about workshops and meetings, and to discuss books and software.

FTP, or File Transfer Protocol, is a tool that lets you transfer files between your computer and another. You'll be able to use your Web browser to copy most files you'll want. However, you may need FTP if you're creating your own Web page or uploading information to someone else's Web site. (See chapter 7.)

Telnet is a tool for accessing programs or databases stored on distant computers. A telnet connection to your office computer, for example, would allow you to sit at home and open spreadsheet, word processing, or other programs that you use at work. Telnet becomes useful if and when you get to the point where you are creating and maintaining your own Web pages. (See chapter 6.) You can also use it to access archives and library catalogs.

SURFING IN
YOUR SLEEP

In the last year or so a number of "offline Web browsers" have been marketed. While your machine is unattended, these software products retrieve updates for Web sites of interest to you. With such products, you can be finding valuable genealogical information while you sleep! The basic idea here is that the files associated with a Web site can be browsed much more quickly if they reside on your own local machine, rather than on some remote server. The actual browsing requires only a click of a mouse—it's the downloading that takes most of the time. So why not do the downloading part while you're not sitting there waiting? When you return to your machine, the Web sites you're following have been updated and are ready for you to browse.

Offline browsers allow you to download entire Web sites, or just the files on the site that have changed since you last checked. Some of them will perform scheduled updates at a day and time you specify. Some may even give you a nice, graphical view of a Web site. For example, the MapViewer feature of FlashSite (InContext

Systems) will show you an entire Web site using differing icons for each type of file, and showing how the files are interrelated. Here is a list of major offline browsers and the URLs at which you can find their developers:

FreeLoader:
  http://www.freeloader.com

Flashed:
  http://www.incontext.com

Internet HotSuite:
  http://www.documagix.com

Lotus Weblicator:
  http://www.lotus.com

NetAttaché Pro:
  http://www.www.tympani.com

Smart Bookmarks:
  http://www.firstfloor.com

Tierra Highlights2:
  http://www.tierra.com

Web Buddy:
  http://www.dataviz.com

WebEx:
  http://www.travsoft.com

WebWhacker:
  http://www.ffg.com

HINTS FOR
SUCCESSFUL SEARCHING

*S*earch engines work by compiling a list of all indexed occurrences of the keywords you typed into a search field. Each of the different engines stores its own database of Internet documents that it knows about. Some of the less powerful ones will only search for keyword occurrences in the titles and headers of documents. More-powerful engines, such as AltaVista, will bring you all occurrences of words throughout a document. The good news is that AltaVista will bring you more documents; the bad news is also that AltaVista will bring you more documents—sometimes more than a million!

And just because a document contains, somewhere within it, all of your search words doesn't mean that it's remotely relevant to your research! Time and practice are the best ways to learn to use search engines effectively, but here are some hints to get you started:

- Be as specific as possible. Typing in keywords, such as "REYNOLDS" and "MASSACHUSETTS," will give a listing of all known Web sites that contain those two words. If the message returns that your search has yielded 179,872 documents, don't be discouraged! Run your search again—but this time, specify "ABRAHAM REYNOLDS," "BOSTON," or "AMERICAN REVOLUTION."

- Try different engines. Search engines maintain databases of all of the Web sites that they know about. But they don't know about a Web site until someone tells the search engines that the site exists— so one engine may yield information that the others don't.

WHAT'S AN
E-MAIL ADDRESS?

Your e-mail address is the Internet equivalent to your phone number: it's a unique identifier that enables people to contact you directly. You can identify an e-mail address at a glance because it always contains this symbol: @, which is read as "at." For example, President Clinton's e-mail address is: *president@whitehouse.gov*.

- *The part preceding the @ is the individual identifier and is usually based on a person's name.*

- *The part following the "@" is the domain name; it often shows the person's school or employer.*

    Many e-mail addresses end in "@aol.com" (for America Online users) or "@compuserve.com" (for CompuServe users).

What Do I Do With These Tools?

There are several ways to use the Internet tools described on pages 31–33 for genealogical research.

Join a mailing list

When you subscribe to a mailing list, such as ROOTS-L, you are basically sharing e-mail with everyone else who subscribes to that list. All of the messages that are posted to the list are delivered to your e-mail box, and any message that you post will be seen by everyone else. According to America Online, there are approximately two thousand mailing lists out there, all organized around particular topics that people like to discuss, from baking bread to managing a health maintenance organization. ROOTS-L, with about 7,500 subscribers, is the oldest and largest mailing list pertaining to genealogy. For a listing of some others, go to http://users.aol.com/johnf14246/gen_mail.html. There, John Fuller has compiled a listing of more than 170 mailing lists on a variety of genealogical topics, from surnames to regions to ethnicities, along with detailed instructions on how to subscribe. Vicki Lindsay also maintains a list of mailing lists at http://www.eskimo.com/~chance/.

WHAT IS A PROTOCOL?

Throughout this book you will see all sorts of acronyms, such as TCP, IP, FTP, POP, PPP, and HTTP. In each of these acronyms, the final "P" stands for "protocol." So what is a protocol?

A protocol is simply a set of rules that two computers follow when communicating. Unlike human communication, which can be imprecise and unclear, computers must communicate in precise, well-defined sequences. For example, one computer might send another a request for information. Such a request has to be in a specified format that the receiving computer knows about. Otherwise, the computer has no way of responding in any useful way. It would be a little like answering the phone, only to hear someone at the other end talking to you in Turkish. Unless you happen to speak Turkish, it's not likely that you'll be able to exchange much information.

The software you run on your computer knows all about these protocols, so you don't have to. You do, however, have to make sure that your software supports all the "right" protocols. For example, if you go the ISP route, your provider is likely to stipulate that you buy software that "uses TCP/IP" which also "supports PPP and POP." (Don't worry about precisely what those terms mean; they're explained elsewhere.) As long as you buy software which provides these features, you're all set. Just install the programs and configure them the way your access provider instructs. . . and you're plugged into the Net! As with most high-tech terminology, the "alphabet soup" of acronyms makes everything sound a lot more complicated than it is!

A mailing list is handled by a host computer, which accepts all incoming mail and then rebroadcasts it to subscribers. One popular program which does this is called "listserv"; hence, the host computers are often called "listservers." Some mailing lists are moderated, which means that a person monitors the list to ensure that all postings are appropriate for the topic of discussion and that no one is behaving improperly by posting personal attacks or deliberately filling the list with inappropriate material. Unmoderated lists do not have such supervision.

All mailing lists work with two separate e-mail addresses. One is the address you use to send messages you want the other readers of the list to see; this is the address you'll use most often as you communicate with other people. The other address communicates with the listserver itself; you use this address only to send basic communications, or commands, to the computer, such as SUBSCRIBE, UNSUB, etc. The latter is the address you will use first, to start receiving mail from the list; thereafter you'll use it only occasionally when you want the computer to adjust your subscription to the list.

For ROOTS-L, the address you use to post messages for other readers is ROOTS-L-@rootsweb.com. The address you use to send commands to the listserver is ROOTS-L-request@rootsweb.com. Be very careful about which address is which! Most mailing lists receive a certain amount of mail that was intended for the listserver but is distributed to the readers instead. And when 7,500 people are

CONTROL YOUR
MAILING LISTS!

Here are a few tips to keep you in control of your mailing lists:

■ Within a few hours of mailing your subscribe command, the listserver will send you a welcome note with detailed instructions on how to use the list, the moderator's policies (if any) about controlling the mail, and a list of commands. Save this message, either on a disk or as a printout in your files; you'll need it.

■ Never send administrative commands to the address you use to post messages to the list. Especially on the larger mailing lists, these unnecessary posts clutter mailboxes and annoy other readers.

■ Instructions for subscribing to mailing lists will often tell you to leave the subject line blank, but some e-mail packages won't send your mail unless you fill in a subject line. Go ahead and put something in the subject line, even if it's just a period. Your own e-mail package will be happy, and the listserver will ignore it.

participating in the discussion, they need to keep the mistakes to a minimum, or everyone will be overwhelmed by useless mail! (See "'Netiquette' Notes," page 44.)

To subscribe to ROOTS-L, send an e-mail to ROOTS-L-request@rootsweb.com with the following line typed into the message: subscribe ROOTS-L [your name]. You should soon receive a welcome note with detailed instructions on how to use the mailing list along with some other commands you can send to the host computer. Here are some of the commands you may find useful:

SET ROOTS-L DIGEST will combine each day's worth of mail into one package to be delivered all at once. The advantage of a digest is that it helps you keep your e-mail organized, especially if you subscribe to more than one mailing list. The disadvantage is that, if you want to save one message in particular, you have to save the entire digest and delete the other messages, or use cut and paste, either of which can become a cumbersome process. Also, if you want to send an individual reply to just one person, you can't just click on REPLY because you'll send the message back to the entire list.

SET ROOTS-L NOMAIL will turn off the mailing list temporarily. You may want to do this if you don't want your e-mail piling up while you're on vacation. SET ROOTS-L MAIL will resume your e-mail delivery.

All of these commands should be sent to the listserver address with no other words in the message field. You're not talking to a human here; you're sending commands to a computer. If you need personal assistance, you should send a private e-mail to the list moderator, whose e-mail address should be included in the welcome note.

Shortly after you subscribe, you should begin receiving e-mail regularly from other subscribers to the list.

Read the newsgroups

Usenet is a vital resource for exchanging information with other genealogists. These newsgroups are similar to mailing lists in that you post messages to a central location where other people can see and respond to them. But they are different in that they aren't delivered to you each day by e-mail; you have to go to them.

SMILE SIDEWAYS!

-mail is everywhere. And once you've used it for awhile, you may wonder how you ever did without it! With it you can convey much more detailed messages than you can with voice mail; you can attach documents and other files; and you never get a busy signal, play phone tag, or interrupt another person's work. You can read your messages at your convenience, and you don't have to wait until business hours to take care of all of your correspondence. Best of all, you can send an e-mail message as far as New Zealand for the price of a local phone call.

And e-mail is evolving into an entirely new form of communication. Because most e-mail messages get deleted as soon as they're read, they're almost as ephemeral as spoken conversation, and people tend to write them more informally than they do memos or even personal letters. But electronic communication lacks the tone of voice, gestures, and facial expressions that communicate as much as your words do when you speak.

Over the years, many shorthand codes have evolved to make e-mail as colorful as conversation. "Smileys," for example, show that you want your comments to be read as humorously or ironically as you meant them. A basic smiley is just a colon and a right parenthesis $\boxed{:)}$; look at it sideways and you see a smiling face.

You'll also see customized smileys. Here's one wearing glasses $\boxed{8)}$; here's a sad face $\boxed{:(}$; this one wears a knowing wink $\boxed{;)}$; this one's laughing $\boxed{:D}$; and this one's sticking out its tongue $\boxed{:p}$. You can also offer a variety of peace offerings, such as a hug $\boxed{\{\}}$ or two $\boxed{\{\{\}\}}$, a kiss $\boxed{\star}$, or a cup of tea: $\boxed{(\_)3}$.

You'll also encounter a number of acronyms that people use as shorthand in e-mail, chats, and postings. Many of these are more common in chat sessions, where you only get to write a few lines at a time. Here are some common ones:

BTW—"By the way."

IMO or IMHO—"In my opinion" or "In my humble opinion."

ROFL—"Rolling on the floor laughing."

TIA—"Thanks in advance."

TTFN—"Ta-ta for now."

The arrangement of postings within each newsgroup will vary depending on the type of software you are using to access them, but the notes will probably be organized chronologically according to the dates they were posted. Behind each note you will find any responses the note might have received.

Most newsreader programs also support "threads." A thread is a sequence of postings to a newsgroup that follow a single line of discussion which originated with one single posting. Some newsreaders, such as *NewsWatcher* for the Mac, will collapse all postings with the same thread into a single line on your screen. By clicking on this line, you can see the entire thread as the discussion unfolded. That way, if you have no interest in the topic, you can easily ignore the entire line.

You can access the newsgroups through your newsreader program or by searching for "usenet" using America Online or CompuServe's internal search programs. Some newsgroups, copied from the America Online search engine, include:

alt.genealogy	soc.genealogy.jewish
soc.genealogy.african	soc.genealogy.medieval
soc.genealogy.australia+nz	soc.genealogy.methods
soc.genealogy.benelux	soc.genealogy.misc
soc.genealogy.computing	soc.genealogy.nordic
soc.genealogy.french	soc.genealogy.slavic
soc.genealogy.german	soc.genealogy.surnames
soc.genealogy.hispanic	soc.genealogy.uk+ireland

You can also find a list of genealogy newsgroups, maintained by John Fuller and Chris Gaunt, at http://www.umich.edu/~cgaunt/gen_intl.html.

Join a BBS

Back in the 1980s, before anyone outside of the government and the universities had ever heard of the Internet, people were already running message board systems called BBSs—bulletin board systems. As the name implies, a BBS is an electronic bulletin board—a central location where you can post messages, and read and respond to messages that other people have posted—just like the newsgroups. The only real difference between the two, to the average user, is that the newsgroups require an Internet connection while the BBSs do not because they are not, in most cases, part of the Internet.

A BBS is sponsored by an individual, known as a systems operator (sysop), who hosts the BBS on his or her own personal computer. Some BBSs are free, but typically you and other subscribers pay that person a fee, as low as $20 per year, in exchange

OUTSIDE LOOKING IN?

*W*hen you plug into the Internet, you gain access to a whole new world (you might say a World Wide Web). But do you also open up your own computer to curious snoopers from every continent? Can other folks browse the data on your computer just as you browse data on the Web? The answer is a definite "No!" All of the information that is available on the Internet is available because someone explicitly placed it there for public perusal. There are three reasons why no one can access your personal computer from the Internet:

■ *In order for your computer to be accessible to a Web browser, your machine has to be configured as an Internet server. When you are browsing the Internet, you are sending requests for data over the phone lines. In order to receive*

requests for data, your computer has to be running specialized software. Unless you run this software, your machine simply cannot accept requests for data.

■ *Your computer is connected to the Net only while you are actually running your TCP/IP software, which manages your Internet session. (A real Web server runs all the time.) When you dial in to the Internet with a typical user account (called a "dial-up PPP" account, or Point-to-Point Protocol), your computer is assigned a temporary IP address (the "handle" that lets one computer access another) only for the duration of your login session. When you log off, your access provider reassigns that number. Because your computer is using this kind of dynamic IP address, there is no fixed address* for the phone number and password to access that BBS computer. You can then dial into that computer and read or download mesages from other subscribers.

Like the newsgroups, BBSs are built around particular discussion topics. There are hundreds of genealogy-oriented newsgroups in towns across the United States as well as several well-known national ones, such as the one run by the National Genealogical Society. You can find a complete list of genealogical BBSs by accessing Richard Cleaveland's list on the NGS home

---■

that uniquely specifies your machine.

All of these account numbers are assigned and reassigned behind the scenes, so you never need to worry about using them. But you should understand that even if people "out there" wanted to see the data on your machine, they wouldn't know where to look because you have a different address each time you log in.

■ *Web servers have to do something that you probably don't do with your own computer:* they have to stay on all the time. *Not only do they have to be powered-on, but they have to be connected to the Internet. Unless your household has a teenager, you probably don't keep your phone lines open twenty-four hours a day.*

You can ask the same question about your television set: "Can other television watchers look into our home through our screen?" Well, first, our televisions are just not equipped to send

images back to the source. Second, since the programs we watch are simultaneously broadcast to millions of households, there is no "pointer" to indicate which set out of all those millions is ours. Finally, when we finish watching the tube, we turn it off. And to carry out our analogy with the Internet fully, we can even unplug the set! (Disconnecting from your access provider accomplishes the same thing as unplugging your set.)

So how does your e-mail find you? It doesn't. Your e-mail is delivered to your mail server—the computer you dial into each time you log on—where it sits waiting for you to come and pick it up. It's sort of like having your mail delivered to a post office box instead of your home; you have to go out to get it.

If you decide that you want *to make information available to others on the Internet, you must first rent storage space on someone else's computer. But as far as your own computer is concerned—not to worry! Big Brother is NOT watching!*

page at http://genealogy.org/~gbbs/.

Although BBSs are not actually part of the Internet, some BBSs now offer you access to the Usenet groups that are on the Internet. Your $20 BBS fee will then give you not only complete e-mail services but also limited Internet access.

After you've been online for awhile, take a close look at your usage. If most of your Internet research centers around the newsgroups, then you may benefit from letting a good BBS connection replace your full Internet service. But you'd be missing out on the resources of the World Wide Web.

"NETIQUETTE" NOTES

I t's hard to hold a conversation with 40 million people. But the Internet is not an anarchy. Most people abide by a set of informal codes of conduct that help to keep the order and make the system run more efficiently. Before you embark on any of the message boards, newsgroups, or mailing lists, please be sure you pay attention to a few brief, common-sense guidelines:

■ **Read the FAQs.** *Long-standing members of discussion groups find it tiresome when new people come in and ask the same basic questions over and over again. Many groups have online archives where you can read older postings and FAQs (Frequently Asked Questions). Reading the FAQs may give you the answers you*

want, and you'll also learn the rules for using the group.

■ **Lurk and listen.** *"Lurkers" are people who listen in on a discussion group without actively participating. If you're new to a discussion, lurking for a few weeks is a good way to get a feel for the personality of the group; you'll gain a better understanding of what the group is about and whether it corresponds to your own interests.*

■ **Keep it short.** *When you do post a query, stick to the subject of the discussion and convey your message as succinctly as possible. No one wants to wade through unnecessary verbiage.*

■ **Don't send attachments to the group.** *If you want to*

What's a Web Page?

Today, the most exciting development on the Internet is the expansion of the World Wide Web. As we discussed in chapter 2, the Web is the "top layer" of the Internet—the part that handles point-and-click interfaces, graphics, and hypertext. There are several concepts you need to learn to understand the Web:

Home pages

Home pages, or Web pages or Web sites, are electronic documents that make up the heart of the Web. These documents are essentially a new form of publishing; anyone with information to share can write it into a home page and place it on a public server

---

share a large chunk of your family history, it may make sense to "attach" a large file of data to your e-mail and post it to the list. Don't. Many people won't be able to read your attachment and won't be able to use it. Even worse, many people have limits on the amount of mail they can receive in a day; if you overload their mailboxes with a large attachment, you can "crash" their mailboxes and cause them to lose all of their mail for the day! The best thing to do is to post a short summary of your ancestors to the list. Anyone who is interested will contact you directly, and you can make private arrangements for sending the larger data file.

- **Send personal messages to people, not groups.** *If you want to respond to a message, but your response would not be of general interest to everyone on the list, send your e-mail directly to that person; do not post it to the list.*

- **Avoid "Me Too" notes.** *If you have something to add to the discussion, by all means, join right in. But imagine if a thousand people all sent messages that said nothing more than "I agree."*

- **Harness your humor.** *"Hey! Knock it off!" Comments like that may be taken as friendly banter when you're speaking, because you can laugh and let the other person know you're teasing. But when you put it in writing, other people won't know whether you're amused, annoyed—or furious. Try to err on the side of caution. And if you do make a comment that you mean to be taken humorously or ironically, show your intentions with a smile!* :) *(See "Smile Sideways!," page 40.)*

open to anyone with Web access.

In the fall of 1996, there were tens of millions of separate documents on the Web, and more are added every day; by the time this book reaches your hands, the number may well be over a hundred million. Taken together, this set of electronic documents is like a giant library of information that exists only on the Internet. Each of those pages was created and placed on the Web for the benefit of people like you.

People create home pages for different reasons. Many companies offer commercial home pages that, just like any other form of advertisement, are designed to sell products or services. Commercial home pages can be from corporations as big and slick as Microsoft or as small and homey as your corner bookstore. Many offer free services to lure you in and keep you coming back.

The federal government has also built many home pages. Many federal publications, from the *Federal Register* to travelers' advisories from the national Centers for Disease Control and Prevention, are available online.

Many home pages are created by nonprofit organizations or professional associations. Health organizations, for example, create home pages to disseminate information and provide support-group connections for people living with anything from AIDS to diabetes to warts.

And many home pages are established by private individuals. Some do it to share their expertise and get in touch with other people interested in the same hobbies or professions. Others are creating their own forum for "sounding off."

Why do people do it? Establishing and maintaining a page on the Web costs time and money. The commercial interests are obviously hoping you'll buy their products and services, but millions of Web pages seem to be there simply to give you free information. Everyone has his or her own reasons, but many are simply seeking contact with other people who have similar interests. You'll find e-mail addresses on many Web pages. If you find a page that is especially useful to you, let the creator know; start a dialogue.

That two-way communication sets the Web apart from any other publishing medium. While you can write a letter to the editor of a newspaper or magazine, the Web is the only place where you can interact directly and immediately with the writer. Even the online forms of the "traditional" publications, such as *National Geographic* or *The Wall Street Journal*, allow for more online feedback that their "dead tree" versions.

⚙ Hypertext

Hypertext is a new concept that also makes Web communication completely unique. When you're reading a document on the World Wide Web, some of the text will appear normally; some will be highlighted in one way or another—it might be underlined or appear in a different color than surrounding text. The highlighted text is "live." That is, if you click on one of these phrases (a link) with your mouse, your browser will transfer you "somewhere else."

That "somewhere else" could take you to another part of the same document or it could take you to Japan or Sweden or Australia. Links are created by the people who write the home pages. Many of them are internal, to connect you to different parts of the same document. Others are external; the creator of the page is showing you other places on the Web that may also interest you.

If we imagine the Web to be a collection of books in a giant electronic library, hypertext is the tool that enables you to jump from book to book as you cross-reference your topics. So you can jump directly to other locations within other documents without having to go through anything analogous to an index or card catalogue.

⚙ HTML

HTML, HyperText Markup Language, is the formatting language that enables those hypertext links to work. The person who creates the Web page needs to write in the commands that tell your browser where to go when you click on the highlighted text. As a browser, you don't need to know too much about how HTML works, but you should understand that HTML is the language that makes the Web run; all documents on the Web use it.

As you can imagine, many people have been making genealogical data available on the Web, and the remainder of this book is dedicated to help you make the most of the genealogical resources that are out there. And, when you're ready to make the step, maybe you'll even write your own home page.

DOCUMENT AT A GLANCE: THE FUTURE

The recent competition between developers of Web browsing software (primarily Netscape and Microsoft) has brought about a remarkable expansion of the capabilities of these browsers. The current generation of browsers will allow you to send and receive e-mail, read newsgroups, and even upload files to host servers.

Most analysts who follow the computer industry believe that the future of document access lies in the seamless integration of editing, desktop publishing, and hypertext browsing software. In such an integrated environment, icons associated with documents will appear on your computer's desktop, just as they do today. However, the distinction between local documents that live on your computer and remote files that may be at the far reaches of the Internet will become obscured. Even today, a browser can format a remote file just as well as it can a local one.

Another distinction that will become less apparent to the user is the difference between being in a browser and an editor or word processor. For example, in Netscape's product Communicator, when you open a document, it asks whether you want to edit it (using Netscape's Composer) or browse it (using Navigator). The editor formats the screen almost exactly as it appears in the browser, but gives you the additional capability of making updates.

Netscape's Communicator will also convert your entire desktop into a browser window. Netscape's integrated environment sits "on top" of the Windows desktop and, to some extent, replaces it. However, Communicator is currently limited in that it only gives you direct access to documents which can be browsed using Navigator; that is, documents written in HTML or the Java language. If you want to view a document written in, say, WordPerfect, you will need to bring it up from your Windows desktop.

It is expected that in the future our computers will let us point and click on any icon we see, and we won't even know (or need to know) what software is being used to present it to us. And since much of this will be accomplished using the Java programming language, which is machine-independent (that is, does not assume any particular hardware manufacturer, such as Intel, Apple, or Motorola), all of our machines may have a very similar "look and feel." So someday you'll be able to sit down at almost any machine—at work or at home— and just click on whatever you see. The software will do the rest!

CHAPTER 4

Where to Dig for Your Cyber-Roots

B Y NOW YOU SHOULD BE COMMUNICATING FREELY WITH GENEALOGISTS THE WORLD OVER, and you should have a rudimentary grasp of navigating on the Web. But the Internet is more than a communications tool; it is also becoming a valuable repository for genealogical data, including searchable databases of surnames and individuals, census data, vital statistics, regional history, and pointers to "conventional" libraries and repositories.

The trick is finding that information and figuring out what to do when you get it. In this chapter, you'll learn:

- *Where to start*
- *How to use source data, such as censuses and vital statistics*
- *How to use search tools to seek out individual genealogies that have been placed on the Net*
- *About regional history societies*
- *How to make visiting libraries, archives, and other "real world" sources easier*

Starting Out

Having access to literally millions of separate documents on the Web is not going to do you any good unless you can find the ones you want. Even your search engines will often bring so many answers to your requests that it's easy to be overwhelmed. That's why many people have created home pages that are essentially directories of useful resources on other Web pages. These people have already done the work of finding, sorting, and alphabetizing hundreds of other pages that they've found to be useful—and now you get to benefit from their work!

By checking out a relatively small handful of very good "compendium" pages, you'll find "ready-to-click" pointers to most of the best that the Web has to offer. Here is a short list of great places to start your own online genealogy hunt:

A Barrel of Links:
> http://cpcug.org/user/jlacombe/mark.html

The Genealogy Home Page:
> http://www.genhomepage.com/

Helm's Genealogy Toolbox:
> http://genealogy.tbox.com/genealogy.html

HINTS FOR FASTER SURFING

Ever heard the term *"World Wide Wait?"* Even with a relatively fast modem, you'll still spend a lot of time waiting for new screens. *The larger the document and the farther away from you it is on the globe, the longer it will take for you to get it. But there are some tricks to speed up your service:*

■ **Log on during off-peak times.** *The more traffic the networks have to handle, the slower the response times get. You'll soon discover that certain hours of the day, like the mid- to late evening, are times when more people are settling down to surf. And when blizzards blanket major regions of the country, millions of bored, snowbound people clog up the*

Genealogy Gateway:
   http://www.polaris.net/~legend/genealogy.htm

Cyndi's List:
   http://www.oz.net/~cyndihow/sites.htm

There are more such pages listed in Appendix A.

Don't forget that the Web is a two-way communications tool. If in your wanderings you run across a page that you think deserves to be included in one of these compendiums, let the page author know!

Vital Statistics

A cornerstone of genealogical research is vital statistics—from the federal censuses to the birth, death, and marriage certificates kept by local and state governments across the nation. The task of converting existing hard copy documents into electronic format is daunting, but the process is well under way. The Web-based researcher finds with each passing month new, online collections of such statistics. We mention only a few here.

-->

Internet. If you are planning to download some large files, schedule some time for yourself during non-peak hours.

■ **Turn off the graphics.** *The more graphic files on a page, and the bigger they are, the longer it will take for you to get the page. But usually, as the page loads, you will see all the text first, and once you can see the words, the hyper-links will work too, even without the graphics. Once you see that you have the text you want, click on STOP; you don't always need to see the pictures.*

You can also select, from your pull-down menu, an option to stop the automatic loading of graphics. Then you'll only see text, unless you decide to view a particular image by clicking on it. Many pages on the Web will also offer you a text-only version.

It may seem nonsensical to praise the graphics capabilities of the Web, and then suggest turning the graphics off. But many Web page creators go over-board and pack their pages with graphics that slow your browsing down without adding any value to your search.

■ *Close any applications you're not actively using. Browsing the Web takes a lot of your computer's memory capacity. To free up more of that memory, try shutting down any programs you may have left running in the background.*

■ *Watch where you're stepping. Accessing documents that reside overseas may take longer. It's not due to the distance itself, since electronic signals travel at the speed of light, but to the number of "nodes," or communications links, between you and the host server. Each signal you send passes*

through a series of hardware devices, and each node has to decide where to forward your signal for the next step in your journey. So the more nodes you use, the more thinking that goes on, and the slower your response gets. So how do you know if you've selected a site from overseas? The clue is in the URL. Most American IP addresses end with a familiar set of three-letter codes. (See "What Is a URL?," page 31.) Many international addresses end in a two-letter

---▶

The history department at the University of Minnesota has placed on the Web a sampling of the U.S. federal census records for 1880. Even though they include data for more than half a million individuals, the sample still represents only 1 percent of the total population for that year. The University of Minnesota data can be found at ftp://ftp.genealogy.org/pub/1880/. You should also retrieve the file called "MUST.HAVE," which describes how the data is arranged and how it can best be obtained.

The National Archives and Records Administration (NARA) offers a guide to census microfilms at http://ftp.genealogy. org/census/contents.html. While this site does not contain any actual census data, it does provide a catalog of available microfilms. You can find what "schedules" are available for the U.S. counties you are searching and exactly which roll of microfilm you need. Additional information is on NARA's own Web page at http://www.nara.gov/.

Mike Gunn of Chatsworth, California, operates another good site that discusses census and Social Security data at http://www.pacificnet.net/~reunions/. You'll find a discussion of the history of the federal, ten-year (decennial) census. His chronology mentions, for example, that the 1850 census was the

country code. This isn't to say that you should never go overseas! Just be prepared to wait a little longer. Here are just a few of the more common codes you may encounter:

au ....Australia
ca .....Canada
ch .....Switzerland
de .....Germany
es .....Spain
fi ......Finland
fr ......France
gr .....Greece
ie .....Ireland

il ......Israel
it ......Italy
jp .....Japan
kr .....South Korea
mx ...Mexico
nl .....Netherlands
no.....Norway
nz ....New Zealand
pl .....Poland
ru .....Russian Federation
se .....Sweden
su .....Soviet Union
tw ....Taiwan
uk ....United Kingdom
us.....United States

first in which the name of every household member was recorded, that most records for 1890 were destroyed in a fire, etc.

If you want to search through a more current census, the home page of the U.S. Census Bureau is at http://www.census.gov/. You can search the 1990 census data by state, county, and district and request to see all sorts of data, such as age, sex, schooling, occupation, salary, etc. This data is available only in summary form, and not by individual household, but modern demographics can often lead to clues about past migrations.

Hamrick Software offers an intriguing free service if you're interested in demographics. Hamrick has collected a database of the 50,000 most common surnames arranged by state. You can enter the surname of interest into a form at their Web site at http://www.hamrick.com/names/; their server will display a map showing the distribution of that name within the United States. Figure 4-1 shows the distribution map for the surname Garretson.

Although Hamrick's maps show only present-day distributions, this figure shows high concentrations of Garretsons in New Jersey, West Virginia, and Wyoming. So one can hypothesize that the Garretsons may have originally settled in New Jersey before moving westward into West Virginia and then on to Wyoming.

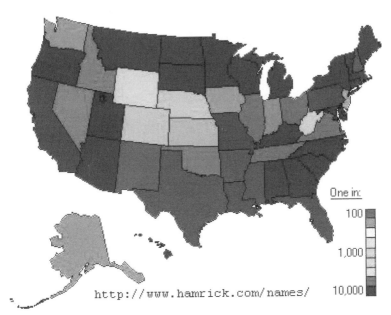

Figure 4-1. Surname Frequency Map
Copyright 1996 Hamrick Software. Used by permission.

Other examples of repositories containing vital statistics are:

Indiana Marriages to 1850:
http://www.statelib.in.us/www.indiana/genealogy/mirr.html

Maine Marriages from 1892 to 1966:
http://www.state.me.us/sos/arc/archives/genealog/marriage.htm

Kentucky Vital Records Collection:
http://ukcc.uky.edu:80/~vitalrec/

British Columbia Vital Record Indexes:
http://www2.bcarchives.gov.bc.ca/textual/governmt/vstats/v_events.htm

American Marriage Records Collection:
http://www.ancestry.com

Pedigrees Across America

Another type of genealogical information on the Web is the rapidly expanding network of personal genealogies that individual

THE MISINFORMATION SUPERHIGHWAY?

A word of caution before you get started. Just because you found the information on the Web does not mean that it's accurate! Always consider the source. If you're retrieving census data from a government site, you can trust it as much as you can any other census data. If, however, you're taking information from a private individual, treat it as you would any other form of secondary information.

Remember that the Web is a new form of publishing but that, instead of going through a publisher, everyone on the Web is essentially self-publishing. So Web publishing is easier than conventional publishing, and the potential for disseminating inaccurate information is greater.

Unlike books or CD-ROMs, a document that resides on the Web can be easily updated. That is, its author can change it any time from the convenience of his or her home. And when a change is made (and then uploaded to the Web server), it is immediately reflected in any subsequent accesses of the document from anywhere in the world. (Try that with paper!) While this powerful capability is exactly what makes the Web so popular and useful, it also has its downside: even the mistakes are immediately broadcast to the four corners of the world. And even if an author notices the mistake, it is impossible to notify everyone who may have already seen and copied the misinformation.

So it's more important than ever to double-check the sources cited by any online genealogy you find. If no source is given, e-mail the author and ask for it. And always remember the adage: "Trust, but verify!"

researchers are putting on the Web. (See "The Misinformation Superhighway?," above.) In the past, people were limited to publishing their research in small quantities from small presses; finding the books you wanted could be very difficult. Now, the Web gives researchers the opportunity to reach a much wider audience much more easily, and it has never been so easy for you to find information from other genealogists.

Perhaps the simplest way to browse genealogies online is to find someone who's already grouped links to a few together onto a single page for you. There are many, many more URLs out there than we can identify here, but here are a few to start with:

http://www.stagedoor.com/gene2.html
http://www.genealogysf.com/gendatus.html
http://genealogy.tbox.com/genealogy/sigen.html
http://www.traveller.com/genealogy/ged2html.htm

All of the above links refer to pages that were created with HTML, the markup language of the World Wide Web. You will also encounter some large repositories of online genealogical data that was contributed by many researchers. Except for GenServ, which is discussed on page 58, the information in these databases is free for the taking. But as a courtesy, you might consider offering in return the results of some of your own research. This voluntary give-and-take is what helps these databases to grow richer all the time. In order for a database like this to work, with information contributed by many different people, all of the information has to be formatted in a common language, GEDCOM. (See "What's GEDCOM?," below.)

Many of the more common genealogy software packages you

WHAT'S GEDCOM?

GEDCOM is the universal language genealogists use to exchange information electronically. GEDCOM, or GEnealogical Data COMmunication, was devised by the Family History Department of The Church of Jesus Christ of Latter-day Saints. The GEDCOM syntax allows a researcher to record names, dates, relationships, and any other desired biographical data using a standard text format. Researchers do not usually read this GEDCOM text directly; they rely on software packages to format it into a more readable (perhaps graphical) form. (For more on genealogical software, see chapter 5.)

The purpose of GEDCOM is to facilitate the exchange of data between researchers who may be using very different computers or software. Each type of computer and software package has its own way of internally repre-

can get today will automatically read GEDCOM data as well as translate your own data into GEDCOM if you choose to transfer what you know into one of these online databases. (See chapter 5 for a closer look at genealogy software.) Here are some online GEDCOM databases:

🌀 **ROOTSBOOK,** maintained by Mickey Lane, is at http://rootsbook.wow.com. ROOTSBOOK is searchable by surname, and you may specify a first initial if you wish to limit your search. Most of these GEDCOM files were donated by individual researchers. For more information on the data you find, you can contact the researcher.

🌀 **Andrew J. Morris** of Farmington, Michigan, maintains a home page at http://genealogy.org:80/~ajmorris/geddex/geddex.htm. This page contains an index of GEDCOM files found on this server. Obtaining these particular GEDCOM files is a two-step process because the files have names such as ab12, aj05, etc. The first step is to identify the name of the file that contains an individual you are interested in. The second step is to download the file having this four-character name. This file

---

senting and storing family history data. There are differing methods of numbering individuals in a database and different methods of establishing links between them. For this reason, it is not generally possible for one researcher to take a family database in "binary" form (that is, a form that is not directly readable by human beings and which has meaning only to the specific hardware and software that created it) and directly transfer it to someone else, unless, of course, the second researcher is using exactly the same type of computer and the same software package.

By converting a database into an intermediate GEDCOM form that is understood by all computers and all software packages, it is possible to exchange data with others—which is what the World Wide Web is all about!

Since the GEDCOM syntax is used only for getting data from "point A" to "point B," it is not necessary that you learn all the ins and outs of the language. It is usually sufficient to know how to tell your software to "export" its database in GEDCOM form. The researcher who receives your data will then do an "import" to get it into the form required by his or her system.

Now you've read that the information on the Web is usually written in HTML, HyperText Markup Language, but that genealogical information is most readily communicated by means of GEDCOM. So you might ask, "Which format do people use to place their genealogies on the Web?" The answer is "Both." Some people export their genealogical databases in GEDCOM format and simply place them on the Web "as is," which means that you have to retranslate them before you can read them. Others convert their GEDCOM files into HTML first, so you can browse them directly.

When you encounter a genealogy in GEDCOM format, you will need to "import" it into one of the many genealogical software packages that are available. If you don't currently use such a package—not to worry! In the

---

will contain GEDCOM data, which you can import into your software package.

🌀 **Gene Stark,** author of the GED2HTML utility described in chapter 6, maintains a Web page from which you can display an automatically generated index of sites that provide genealogies in a particular format. This format is nonstandard, but his GED2HTML utility supports it. Even though the format is not universally accepted, there are a fair number of genealogies accessible from his index. His page is at http://bsd7.cs.sunysb.edu/~stark/genweb_index/Welcome.html.

🌀 **GenServ** is a very large genealogical database with more than 6,800,000 names. The database is usually accessed by e-mail, and the price of gaining access to GenServ is to submit a GEDCOM file containing data from your own research and to pay an annual fee of $12. After you have done this, you can use a specified e-mail address to request information on surnames. Within an hour or so, you will get an e-mail response listing all occurrences of that name. For example, the command "search: yeager" would yield a list of all individuals GenServ knows about with the surname YEAGER and the specific user database which contains the entry. If you find an individual who interests you, you can request a full report on

next chapter we'll list some of these packages and tell you how you can get them. You'll probably find a software product that will be to your liking. It's fairly difficult to read a GEDCOM file directly, so you will pretty much need to rely on software to make heads or tails of it. If you don't want to do this type of import, another option would be to convert the GEDCOM into HTML and browse it with your Web browser. (See chapter 6.)

In the early days of HTML, some people put their genealogies online by creating HTML documents from scratch, using a word processor or text editor. Perhaps the best known and largest of these is the Churchyard/Orr genealogy, at http://uts.cc.utexas.edu/~churchh/chrchyrd.html. The current trend, however, is to use software to convert GEDCOM files into HTML automatically. You'll learn more about this process in chapter 6. For now, just be aware that you will find genealogies in both formats.

that person by sending another note.

You can request that your report be produced in any of several different formats. The response also contains the name and address of the researcher who provided the information. While GenServ doesn't allow you to download any GEDCOM files, and it doesn't let you browse genealogical data interactively, the database is big enough to be useful. For more details about the service, visit the home page at http://soback.kornet.nm.kr/~cmanis/. GenServ lets you do a one-time, online search before becoming a member, just to see what they're all about.

If you don't see a surname of interest in one of these genealogy databases, you will want to search for it using one of the many Web-based search engines. Chapter 3 discussed search engines, such as AltaVista, Yahoo!, and WebCrawler, that will point you to all Web pages (or newsgroups) they know about regardless of content. (See "Hints for Successful Searching," page 35.) Keep in mind that these engines are not specialized for genealogy. For example, if you ask AltaVista to show you a list of all Web pages containing the phrases "Blankenship family" and "genealogy," you get just that—nothing more. You will not get occurrences of variant spellings such as Blankinship with an "i," and you will not get occurrences of "Blankenship family" with "pedigree." This is in contrast to some software packages, such as that used to search the International Genealogical Index (IGI) CDs, which will display variant spellings of a requested surname. (IGI software us used in LDS family history centers and some other libraries. If you use it search for a particular surname, such as Rogers, you will receive a list that includes variant spellings, such as Rodgers.)

Seeking Regional History

Although people tend to emphasize the global proportions of the World Wide Web, it can also be an important source for local and regional histories. And getting in touch with people online sure beats flying across the country—or across the ocean—every week.

And even if exploring local history doesn't yield new data, just learning what life was like one or two hundred years ago gives you perspective on your ancestors' lives. Sometimes we get so involved in trying to find birth dates or maiden names that it's easy to forget that the country may have been in the midst of a civil war at the time! (This is why some genealogical software products chart lifespans on a historical time line—so that it all stays in perspective.)

Not surprisingly, a number of Web pages are dedicated to regional history. Pay a visit to Helm's Genealogy Toolbox at http://genealogy.tbox.com/genealogy/area.html for an excellent pointer to many state, local, and special-interest historical societies. For example, check out the Allegheny Regional Family History Society page at http://www.swcp.com/~dhickman/arfhs.html. The page, maintained by Deborah Hickman, focuses on family history and genealogy throughout the Allegheny Mountain region. In addition to family histories, it also features articles describing life in earlier times in the region.

Many sites are dedicated to providing historical information on specific countries or regions within countries. For example, check out the home page for the Irish Family History Foundation at http://www.mayo-ireland.ie/roots.htm. From here, you can browse family history information for counties Clare, Kilkenny, or Limerick (as well as most of the other counties). But for Americans, browsing pages from the Old World may raise more questions than answers. You can find out where (and how) people sharing your surname lived in the "mother country," but you're on your own to find the immigration links.

Unfortunately, you won't yet find much "hard" information online relating to immigration (for example, passenger lists), probably because the sheer number of immigrants to the U.S. is so large that any attempt at establishing a comprehensive, systematic, online database has been prohibitive. One day this may become possible as data rates and the capacities of storage devices continue to increase. For now, you can find some limited immigration information on the Web for selected nationalities or regions. For example, the Pennsylvania Chapter of the Palatines to America has set up a page at http://genealogy.org/%7Epalam/ia_index.htm. This page will also allow you to add your own immigrant ancestor. Another page, at http://members.aol.com/calebj/mayflower.html, contains genealogical information on the Mayflower passengers.

Sometimes ethnic or religious links are grouped together with area-specific pages. Matt Helm does this in his Genealogy Toolbox at http://genealogy.tbox.com/genatl/genatl.htm. He has a number of links for Jewish and Quaker genealogy, which he places on a page with regional pointers.

Pointers to the "Real World"

Try as you might, it still isn't possible to do *all* of your research through the convenience of your computer. Sometimes, you just have to venture out into the real world to visit libraries, archives, historical societies, and courthouses. But here, too, the Web can help simplify your life. Many libraries will post their hours and policies online, allowing you to plan your trip before you go. Sometimes you can even learn whether the book you want is at the library before you waste time driving there to find out that you can't find what you want. For example, the Library of Congress's card catalog is online in an HTML search engine, so when you arrive you already know where to go to find what you want. Many libraries provide catalogs of their holdings through a telnet login. A good starting point to see what online catalogs are available in your region is Stanford University's LibWeb site, at http://sunsite.berkeley.edu/Libweb/.

You might even learn about small but rich libraries, bookstores, etc., that are located nearby—and that you won't even know about until you find them online. For example, the National Genealogical Society has an excellent library in Arlington, Virginia, but because it's hidden from the main road, it would be easy to drive right past without ever knowing it was there! But the NGS home page, at http://genealogy.org/NGS/welcome.html, will tell you about the library's holdings, its recent acquisitions, its hours, and even where you can park.

Here are a few pages to help you start finding libraries and archives:

Genealogical Archives and Libraries:
http://www.everton.com/archives.html

A VIRTUAL SHOPPING SPREE!

Some of the more "excited" hype about the wonders of the Internet has heralded the joy of online shopping malls. Well, guess what? Online shopping is a lot of fun, and it's also a great way to get your hands on some rare, out-of-print, and other hard-to-find books, not to mention other genealogical tools and supplies. You can search the databases of books through several specialist outlets, some of which offer online ordering forms, and within a few weeks the genealogy book you've sought all your life is on its way to your door.

A good place to start looking for books is Amazon.com, Inc., at http://www.amazon.com/. *Amazon has a very friendly and sophisticated series of HTML forms for searching its bookshelves (by author, title, or subject), reading a short summary of the book, checking its availability, and placing the order. Amazon does not specialize in genealogy, but it does stock well over 2 million (yes, million) books, so you will find a good selection of all types of books—both in-print and out-of-print.*

If you don't find it at Amazon, check out one of the booksellers that does specialize in genealogical, historical, or antiquarian books. A few of them are:

Public Access Library Catalogs (dialup and telnet):
 http://www.genealogy.org/~ngs/dialup.html

Libweb:
 http://sunsite.berkeley.edu/Libweb/

U.S. National Archives:
 http://www.nara.gov/

This chapter has offered you a few drops in the ocean of information you can find on the World Wide Web. The Web gives you access to much more information—much faster—than any phone book. And you can access this information anytime you want to see it. And the Web is constantly changing and growing. So keep "surfing." You never know what might turn up!

--➤

Antiquarian Booksellers:
 http://www.abaa-booknet.com/
Zarahemla Book Shoppe:
 http://www.xmission.com/~zarahmla
Frontier Press:
 http://www.doit.com/frontier/
Blair's Book Service:
 http://www.genealogy.com/blairs
Willow Bend Books:
 http://server.mediasoft.net/ScottC
Ancestry Incorporated:
 http://www.ancestry.com/

In addition, you can buy CD-ROMs containing genealogical data that ranges from censuses to marriage, birth, and death archival records. Several online vendors sell genealogical CD-ROMs:

Banner Blue:
 http://www.familytreemaker.com
Global Heritage Center:
 http://www.ledet.com/genealogy

Everton Publishers:
    http://www.everton.com/ecdcat.html
Heritage Books, Inc.:
    http://www.heritagebooks.com
Automated Research, Inc.:
    http://www.aricds.com/products.html
AGLL Genealogical Services:
    http://www.agll.com/elect/el.html

Or, if you're more into microfiche:

Ancestor Publishers:
    http://www.firstct.com/fv/ancpub.html
A. J. Morris Genealogy:
    ftp://genealogy.org/~ajmorris/catalog/catalog.htm

For other genealogical supplies—binders, charts, maps, guides, even bumper stickers ("Genealogists Dig Their Roots")—here are a few more sites to visit:

Genealogy Unlimited, Inc.:
    http://www.itsnet.com/home/genun/public_html/
Everton Publishers:
    http://www.everton.com/
SGS Genealogical Supplies:
    http://spider.regina.ism.ca/orgs/sgs/supplies.htm

You may want to be cautious about sending anyone your credit card number over the Internet! *Your number can fall into unauthorized hands no matter how you use it these days—by mail, phone, or even face-to-face sales in a store—but Internet commerce is still young, and vendors are still figuring out how to handle this problem. Although there are "secure" protocols that can be used with a Web browser to ensure that only you and the vendor see this information, there is some controversy over just how secure these methods are. Most vendors will allow you to use another payment method—by calling or faxing in your credit card number or even snail-mailing a check.* Caveat Surfor!

CHAPTER 5

Genealogy Software on the Web

I NDEX CARDS, BINDERS, FILE FOLDERS, AND REAMS OF PAPER
HAVE LONG BEEN THE GENEALOGIST'S LOT IN LIFE. But your
computer offers you a great opportunity to develop a new system—one that will keep your notes neat, organized, and leg-
ible, even when your ancestor list grows into the hundreds or
thousands.

Also, because you'll be downloading information from the
Web in electronic formats, it'll actually be easier to continue to
store the data on your computer than to print it out and transfer
it to your cards.

Fortunately, you don't have to spend a lot to get some excellent genealogy programs. Although several commercial genealogy
software packages are available in most software stores, this chapter discusses only software that is available on the Web. Most of
these packages are available free of charge or are very inexpensive.

This chapter will help you find the software that is right for
you. You'll learn:

- *What shareware and demonstration software are*
- *How to select software products that suit your needs*
- *How to find and download software off the Web*

What Is Shareware?

Many of the software packages discussed in this chapter fall in the category of shareware. "Shareware" describes software that is offered to the general public on a trial basis at little or no cost with the understanding that anyone who decides to use the product regularly will send a specified, modest registration fee to the author, at the address shown on the program. This software is usually written by people who have a passion for the topic at hand and who didn't write the product with an eye toward making a great deal of money. For this reason, the cost of a shareware product is typically a fraction of its commercial counterpart.

Quality varies. Sometimes shareware is a perfectly adequate substitute for an expensive commercial product. And sometimes you'll get a real gem, created by a programmer with an in-depth understanding of the topic; it'll beat anything else you could possibly buy. But even if you get something you don't like at all, you haven't lost anything.

The shareware marketplace relies on "the honor system." While shareware police won't come around to your house to make sure you paid for your products, it is expected that regular users send in the requested amounts, which can be as low as $5 to $10. The authors usually use this revenue to defray the costs of writing and distributing the product, and "registered" users frequently receive free upgrades, support, and additional documentation (sometimes hard-copy manuals).

Often the software itself is written so that registered users have access to additional features not available to the "casual downloader." But perhaps the best reason to mail the payment is simply to say "Thank you" to a fellow genealogy enthusiast for making your hobby more enjoyable and to give him or her an incentive to keep working on better and stronger products.

Demonstration software is different. Sometimes manufacturers of commercial software will place demonstration ("demo") copies of their products on the Web. Demo software differs from shareware in that:

❋ **Demo versions are more limited.** By severely limiting the capabilities of a demo version, a commercial developer ensures that no one will be able to use the product without buying a bona fide copy.

❋ **Commercial software costs more.** Recently, the distinction between shareware and commercial products has begun to blur. Shareware marketing is becoming more sophisticated, and the costs of registration are increasing. At the same time, commercial software developers, once known for their steadfast insistence on payment *up front,* are serving up their products on the Web for widespread examination. (In fact, Netscape uses this approach for its Web browser *Navigator.* You can get *Navigator* from the Web, which can be cumbersome, since it's a fairly large file. Or you can buy it in the store, which will also give you manuals and documentation.)

What to Look For in Software

Every researcher has different priorities and techniques. And each software package has its unique strengths and weaknesses. So before you commit your life's work to any one package, you will want to do some of your own comparative shopping and make sure that the product has the features that YOU need. Here are some important questions to ask yourself:

❋ **Will I be sharing data with other genealogists?** If you expect to retrieve genealogical data from the Web, or to share your work with others, the ability to import and export GEDCOM files is vital.

❋ **What kind of trees do I want to use?** Not all software will generate trees of both ancestors and descendants. Also check to see whether the trees can be traversed interactively or whether each tree has to be generated individually.

❋ **Does this package organize data the same way I do?** Some software displays database records that look just like index cards; others talk about life "events" and arrange them chronologically.

VIRUS ATTACK!
OR "BEWARE OF COMPUTER GEEKS BEARING GIFTS"

When you're downloading executable programs, you need to beware of possible infection by a computer virus—a program that copies itself from one diskette to another, or from one computer to another. Viruses are written by overzealous computer programmers who are either very bored or who want to prove to the world how clever they are. Although computer viruses are given cute or whimsical names like Yankee Doodle, Music Bug, Cinderella, or Frere Jacques, they are far from amusing, especially if you happen to be the one whose system is infected by one.

All viruses have one thing in common—they are designed to reproduce themselves and spread to other computers. Beyond that, they come in all "shapes and sizes," some of which are dangerous, some of which are not. Some viruses attach themselves to your hard disk so that you run the virus program every time you turn your computer on. Others attach themselves to executable files, such as DOS files ending in .EXE or .COM, and run only when you activate those files. Some viruses copy themselves precisely, while others create slightly different (but still active) versions of themselves each time they reproduce.

So what exactly does a virus do, other than reproduce itself? In some cases, nothing. There are a number of viruses that simply copy themselves from disk to disk, and do nothing more. This may seem harmless, but it can eat up space on your disks, take up memory which other programs need to run, and slow your computer down. More mischievous viruses will also display flashy messages, cause the system to beep, lock up the keyboard, or otherwise wreak havoc. Of course, the most dangerous viruses are those that cause irreversible damage to your system, such as formatting your hard disk (which permanently wipes out all files that were stored on it).

Your system can become infected when you boot with an infected floppy disk or when you execute a program containing a virus. How will you know that your machine is sick? In most cases, you won't—at least not right away. A virus can be diligently copying itself at the same time you are running your software, and there may be no visible sign that anything is wrong. Some virus programs remain dormant until a specific date or time to "trigger" their most malicious deeds. For example, there is a "Christmas Virus" that infects ".COM" files. If an infected program is executed during the Christmas season (between December 24 and January 1), it displays a picture of a Christmas tree. So far, it's only moderately annoying. But if an infected program is run on April 1 (of any year), it destroys the data on your hard disk! So if your computer was infected with a Christmas Virus on April 2, you would have no idea that anything was wrong for almost nine months!

So what's a modern-day, turn-of-the-millennium computer genealogist to do? While downloading files right and left, can you be sure that none of them has any viruses lurking in it? The short answer is "No." But you can take steps to minimize the chance that your system might be compromised. Many vendors sell anti-virus software, which you can find in your local computer store. Typically, this type of software activates every time you start your computer, and at least part of the program remains "resident" in memory (i.e., continues to run in the background) to make sure that you don't contract any computer viruses during your session.

Not surprisingly, anti-virus programs are also available on the Net. Several good programs can be found at the TUCOWS (pronounced "two cows!") collection of Internet software. Its URL

is http://www.sasknet.com/~tucows/. In particular, you might want to check out Thunderbyte Anti-Virus or Mcafee Viruscan. These are both available from TUCOWS, but they also have their own Web pages at http://www.thunderbyte.com and http://www.mcafee.com, respectively.

Unfortunately, since the list of computer viruses is always growing, there is no way that anti-virus packages can recognize every virus that might come along. That is why many manufacturers of anti-virus products have a policy of periodically updating their customers' software or databases. As new viruses are discovered, the anti-virus package is updated too. Unfortunately, the virus writers are always one step ahead, since a virus has to be discovered before an effective "treatment" can be developed. In this respect, computer viruses are very much like biological viruses.

If you buy one of the anti-virus packages, hopefully you won't be one of the few to see a message like "HA HA HA YOU HAVE A VIRUS." But what if you don't buy anti-virus software, and you do see a message such as the above (or any other peculiar behavior, such as screen flickering, extreme system sluggishness, or unusually large memory utilization)? Turn your computer OFF! It is not sufficient to do a "warm boot," such as the Ctrl-Alt-Del key sequence in DOS, since some viruses can live *through such a boot. You should not turn your computer on again until you have placed a bootable diskette (preferably one that contains an anti-virus program) into your floppy drive. The diskette should have its write-protect slider set to the "protect" position. Otherwise, after you boot, the virus may just infect the new diskette the same way it did your hard disk. Furthermore, the diskette should be one that you haven't booted with recently, since it would most likely have the virus on it as well.*

Of course, there's no need to sound the alarm and reach for the "virus vaccine" disk every time your system slows down. Software today is very graphics intensive, and programs such as Web browsers can use a fair chunk of memory. Also, be aware that by far the greatest contributor to your response time while surfing the Net is your modem (and any other machines between you and the Web server). So there will be times when your system will not be lightning-fast. A good rule of thumb is to close any programs that might be run-

ning in the background. If you're surfing the Net right now, there's no particular reason to keep that spreadsheet program around. And just minimizing the icon doesn't help. You need to actually end the program, so it frees up any system resources (memory, disk space) that it may have had locked. If this doesn't help, you might try re-booting your system. This will return your system to its original state, with its full complement of memory and disk space. If the problem persists, and if the same software ran just fine yesterday, you probably want to look into it further. It's unlikely that your problem will be due to a virus. It may just be that your system needs some fine tuning.

Finally, we should point out that not all harmful programs of this type are viruses. Technically, in order for a program to be a virus, it has to reproduce itself. But it's possible for any program to do just as much damage. For example, there are programs called "Trojan horses" which do something very different than they claim to do. The program might claim to be some

-->

🔁 **Do I want to incorporate electronic photographs?** What about electronic images of individuals, maps, letters, wills, or deeds? Some excellent databases don't handle images at all. Others are excellent photo archives but poor for storing large amounts of biographical data. (See "Do I Want a Scanner?," page 72.)

🔁 **Do I mind juggling complex numbering systems?** Some packages force you to use Record Identification Numbers for

friendly utility, such as a disk management program. But when you run it, you
could find out that it is actually a disk
scrambling program. Such programs
don't need to attach themselves to a disk
or an executable file in order to run. You
run them yourself—voluntarily! Unfortunately, there's not a whole lot that can
be done about this type of deception. Here
some steps you should take before you run
a program that you have downloaded:

■ **Read the documentation
  carefully.** If you see any indica-
  tion that the program might not be
  authentic, DO NOT run it.
  Authors of Trojan horse programs
  sometimes put in hints, perhaps in
  the belief that no one actually reads
  program documentation.

■ **Download only from FTP
  sites that you know to be
  reputable.** For example, you
  could use a site that you have used
  before. Or if members of a newsgroup
  or mailing list have recommended a
  particular program from a certain site,
  you should find it safe, too. You

might even ask others where
they got their version of a program,
and whether they are running anti-
virus software.

If you download often, you might
periodically read one of the newsgroups
relating to computer security, to make
sure that there are no new Trojan horses
out there. To find out more about
viruses, including bulletins describing
recent "strains," check the Web pages at:

Symantec AntiVirus
Research Center
http://www.symantec.com/avcenter/

Data Fellows Online
Virus Database
http://www.DataFellows.com/vir-info/

There's no reason to avoid
the Internet for fear of viruses.
Most system administrators are
very careful to check the programs on
their Web servers before they become
available to the public.

The best approach is simply to
buy an anti-virus package and . . .
Enjoy the Net!

-----

each individual in your database. Others "hide" the numbers
and let you deal only with the names. (After all, isn't that what
computers do best—keep track of tedious lists of numbers so
we humans don't have to?)

How much control do I want over the output—charts,
text reports, GEDCOM? Some packages give you more
capability to edit the particular data that appears when you
print a chart. For example, you may or may not want the cur-

DO I WANT
A SCANNER?

Electronic databases give you a new option for those family photos, not to mention maps, certificates, and other fragile documents: electronic storage and display. But getting those pictures online isn't as easy as typing a paragraph; you need access to a scanner. Some photocopying centers also offer scanning services, which may be your best bet if you only want to scan a maximum of four or five images. But if you want more, consider purchasing a scanner:

■ A *flatbed* scanner—which looks somewhat like a photocopier, with a flat glass scanning area and a plastic cover—will give you the best quality pictures. Drawbacks: The flatbeds take up a lot of table space, and at up to $1,000, they're expensive.

■ A *combination* scanner—one piece of equipment that serves as printer, phone, fax machine, answering machine, and scanner—

can save space in your office. Drawbacks: You have to feed the original through a slot, like you do on a fax machine, which means that you can't scan from books. These machines cost between $500 and $1,000.

■ A *hand* scanner—a small, handheld device that looks somewhat like a giant mouse—is the most inexpensive option, for under $300. Drawbacks: Because you move it by hand, it can be difficult to get a straight picture. You can buy trays to help align the scanner as it moves, but that doesn't help with books.

Another option to consider with some scanners is color. While most of the photographs and other images genealogists encounter are likely to be black and white, you may still want to be able to scan color images on occasion. (See chapter 6 for tips on creating graphics files.)

rent date to appear at the top of the page. Or you may not want christening data on your pedigree charts.

🌀 **How good is the search capability?** As new data filters in, you will spend a lot of time "hopping" from one record to another. The more cumbersome that process, the more quickly you'll get annoyed. Some programs feature sophisticated search capabilities that let you find a record with a few keystrokes.

🌀 **How many records do I need to store?** If you have a large database, you can rule out some programs immediately. Also be aware that a theoretical upper limit on the number of records may be different than the maximum number that can be conveniently accessed. A large database may slow a program down so much that it's too hard to use. To check this, import a large GEDCOM file into a demo copy of the software and see what happens.

Software You Can Get From the Web

Perhaps the best place to start your Web search for genealogy software is the Web site "Genealogy Software Springboard" at http://www.toltbbs.com/~kbasile/software.html. This site contains links to a number of popular genealogy products, along with reviews provided by users. It contains lists of software features provided by the developers, as well as announcements of anticipated future releases.

By browsing the above Web site, you can read reviews, download shareware or demonstration copies of the products, and decide which of the products will best suit your needs.

In the following tables are summarized some of the genealogical shareware and demo software available on thc Web. We should note that one of the key software products used by genealogists, *Personal Ancestral File (PAF)*, is not available on the Web. For information on PAF, you can check out the PAF Review Web page at http://www.genealogy.org/~paf/, or contact your local LDS family history center. Very often these centers have a copy of PAF installed on a computer for public use. A PAF session at one of these workstations may help you determine whether

PAF is the right package for you, or whether one of the following might be more to your liking.

Software for IBM-PC and Compatibles

Reunion:
http://www.LeisterPro.com/

The Master Genealogist:
http://www.WhollyGenes.com/

Brother's Keeper:
http://web.wingsbbs.com/brotherskeepr/

Family Origins:
http://www.parsonstech.com/genealogy/

Family Gathering (Mac also):
http://www.palladiumnet.com/palladium.html

Family Tree Maker (Mac also):
http://www.familytreemaker.com/

Ancestral Quest:
http://www.ieighty.net/~ancquest/

WinGen:
http://www.shareware.com/

Family Tree in a Window:
http://www.shareware.com/

Genius for Windows:
http://ourworld.compuserve.com/homepages/re scho/

Corel Family Publisher:
http://www.progeny2.com/

Software for the Macintosh

Reunion:
http://www.LeisterPro.com/

Gene:
http://www.ics.uci.edu/~epstein/gene/

Heritage:
http://www.eskimo.com/~grandine/heritage.html

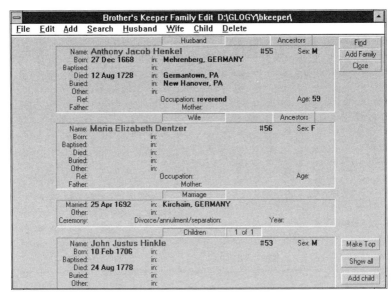

Figure 5-1. The Edit Screen in *Brother's Keeper*
Used by permission.

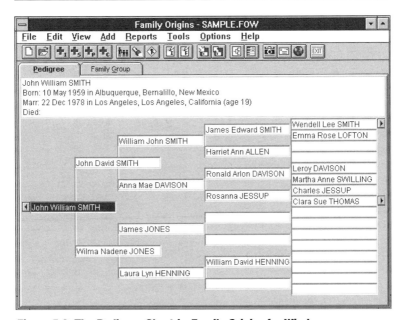

Figure 5-2. The Pedigree Chart in *Family Origins* for Windows
Copyright 1996 by Parsons Technology. All rights reserved. Used by permission.

REPORT FORMATS
AND NUMBER SYSTEMS

Through the years, genealogists have used several numbering systems to identify individuals in printed reports and books. As you might expect, today's genealogy software has adopted these numbering systems to identify individuals in databases. Whatever method you used to keep your records in the past, when you start dealing with computer-based systems in your home or on the Internet, you'll be working with at least one of these systems.

Here are the three most widespread numbering systems in use today. Two of them are used when reporting on descendants; the other is for ancestors. Each numbering scheme has its advantages and disadvantages.

Descendants:
The Register Systems

There are two variations of the so-called "register" system, developed by the New England Historic Genealogical Society. In the basic register system, the children within a family are assigned Roman numerals, but are assigned Arabic numerals only if they had offspring. For example:

1. Joseph Patrick Kennedy,   b. 6 Sep 1888,   m. 7 Oct 1914
   Rose Elizabeth Fitzgerald,   b. 22 Jul 1890,   d. 22 Jan 1995.
   Joseph died 18 Nov 1969.

   Children:
   i   Joseph Patrick Kennedy Jr., b. 25 Jul 1915, d. 12 Aug 1944.
2. ii   John Fitzgerald, b. 29 May 1917.
   iii   Rosemary (Rose Marie) Kennedy, b. 20 Feb 1920.
   iv   Kathleen "Kick" Kennedy, b. 20 Feb 1920, m. 6 May 1944
         William John Robert Cavendish, b. 10 Dec 1917, d. 10 Sep 1944.
         Kathleen died 13 May 1948.
3. v   Eunice Mary   b. 10 Jul 1921.
4. vi   Patricia   b. 6 May 1924.
5. vii   Robert Francis   b. 20 Nov 1925.
6. viii Jean Ann   b. 20 Feb 1928.
7. ix   Edward Moore   b. 22 Feb 1932.

In the modified register (or "record") system, all offspring are assigned numbers (both Arabic and Roman) and plus signs are used to indicate which of them continued their lines with further offspring:

1. Joseph Patrick Kennedy,   b. 6 Sep 1888, m. 7 Oct 1914
    Rose Elizabeth Fitzgerald, b. 22 Jul 1890, d. 22 Jan 1995.
    Joseph died 18 Nov 1969.

    Children:
    2.   i   Joseph Patrick Kennedy Jr., b. 25 Jul 1915, d. 12 Aug 1944.
    +3.   ii   John Fitzgerald b. 29 May 1917.
    4.   iii   Rosemary (Rose Marie) Kennedy, b. 20 Feb 1920.
    5.   iv   Kathleen "Kick" Kennedy, b. 20 Feb 1920, m. 6 May 1944
            William John Robert Cavendish, b. 10 Dec 1917,
                 d. 10 Sep 1944.
            Kathleen died 13 May 1948.
    +6.   v   Eunice Mary   b. 10 Jul 1921.
    +7.   vi   Patricia   b. 6 May 1924.
    +8.   vii   Robert Francis   b. 20 Nov 1925.
    +9.   viii   Jean Ann   b. 20 Feb 1928.
    +10.   ix   Edward Moore   b. 22 Feb 1932.

As you read further into such a report, you know that any additional offspring you find should be associated with individuals who had a plus sign next to their entry. This lets you find the right person at a glance.

Of course, since the modified register system assigns Arabic numbers to everyone, some of these numbers are never referenced from any point in the text—there are no offspring paragraphs to refer back to them. Strictly speaking, there is no reason ever to print out such an unused number. The number may be of use to database software, however, because computers need these "handles" to access the individual's record. Even we humans may find these seemingly extraneous Arabic numbers useful if we wish to identify an individual as being someone's uncle, cousin, etc., or if we have other life events we wish to record. Furthermore, if we leave these numbers out (i.e., if we use the basic, unmodified register system), it may be confusing if some of the siblings in a family have Arabic numbers, while others have only Roman numbers. It may give the impression that the siblings belong to different generations.

Ancestors:
The Ahnentafel System

The ahnentafel system is used almost exclusively as the method for numbering ancestors. (Ahnentafel is the German word for "ancestor table," or list of ancestors.) The main reason for this is its straightforwardness. An individual of interest (often, the compiler of a genealogy) is given the number 1. His father is assigned the number 2; his mother, 3. In general, a person's father will have a number that is twice that of the offspring; the mother will have a number one greater. This simple, recursive definition allows a computer program or a human being to quickly and easily determine the ahnentafel number of anyone in a genealogy.

Here's the same example, this time going backwards in time:

1. John Fitzgerald Kennedy

Parents
2. Joseph Patrick Kennedy
3. Rose Elizabeth Fitzgerald

Grandparents
4. Patrick Joseph Kennedy
5. Mary Augusta Hickey
6. John Francis "Honey Fitz" Fitzgerald
7. Mary Josephine Hannon

Of course, the ahnentafel numbering system won't work for numbering descendants or ancestors' siblings. When we are traversing the family tree backward through the generations, each branch in the tree splits off in precisely

---

The Incredible Expanding Software

Before you can download and use most software on the Web you have to "uncompress" it. You're familiar with the term "Some Assembly Required"? Software programs tend to come in very large files and, like your office furniture, it is disassembled, or "compressed," for more efficient delivery, and has to be "decompressed," or reassembled, before you can use it. This technique of software compression allows you to retrieve files faster, and it also keeps Web traffic to a minimum.

It's possible that your Web browser is already configured so that it will decompress your software automatically as you download it.

two directions—fraternal and maternal. But when moving forward chronologically, the number of branches (siblings) will be different in each family. So there is no way to uniformly describe how the tree is laid out.

Of course, there are also some drawbacks to the ahnentafel system. Since there are twice as many people in each receding generation, the number associated with ancestors in distant generations can be unwieldy. And unless your genealogy is more complete than most, you probably have no information about the individuals in many of these slots. So you'll have a lot of (very large) unused numbers. Handling these useless numbers used to be a problem for home computers, since it was difficult to get enough memory to store this information. But today's home computers are much faster, have much more memory, and can access much more stored data (hard disks, CD-ROMs) than even large "mainframe" computers could only a few years ago.

The other problem with ahnentafel numbers is that they are associated with positions in the ancestral tree, not individuals. If an individual occurs in more than one position in the tree, he or she will have two different ahnentafel numbers. This may be acceptable for human beings—perhaps even desirable, since each number tells us which line we are interested in. But for computers, each record in a database must have a unique identifier. There are two solutions to this problem. One is to keep two actual database records for the "double ancestor"—one record for each ahnentafel number. The other solution is to keep the actual data in only one place and somehow keep track of the fact that two different ahnentafel numbers point to it. In either case, this is something that only your database program has to worry about. The only thing you need to worry about is how you're going to find information for all those empty slots in the tree!

Most recent browsers have option screens that will let you specify "helper applications." These are separate programs to which incoming files can be passed for some sort of additional processing, such as decompression. In this case, you would "magically" find the complete software package you wanted all ready to roll.

If your browser doesn't offer that option, no problem. You need to run a simple program to decompress those files, and you can find the decompression software (where else?) on the Web. The two most popular forms of data compression are "zip" (for IBM-PCs and compatibles) and "StuffIt archive" (for Apple Macintoshes). Files compressed using these techniques are usually given names ending in ".ZIP" and ".sit," respectively.

The .ZIP utilities are *PKZIP* for DOS and *WinZip* for Windows. You can find these at the home page for PKWARE Inc., http://www.pkware.com/Welcome.html. For .sit files, you will want to retrieve *StuffIt Expander*, developed by Aladdin Systems Inc., from http://www.aladdinsys.com/consumer/. There is also a version of *Stuffit Expander* for Windows at this site.

Here is how you would go about downloading from the Web a file which has been compressed:

- When you find a hypertext link that points to one of these files, click on it to copy ("download") it to your home computer.

- If your browser can't figure out how to decompress the file for you, it will leave a file with an extension of ".ZIP" or ".sit" on your hard drive.

- If you are using Windows 95 or a Macintosh, the newly downloaded file will probably appear on your desktop as a *WinZip* or *StuffIt Expander* icon. This means that when you double-click on it, the decompression program will automatically place the fully-expanded files in the directory or folder you specify. (Even if a different icon appears on your compressed file, the *WinZip/Stuffit* utilities can be used to decompress it, provided that you run/launch the utility separately, and then open the compressed file from a menu option.)

- If you are working in a DOS Window, you would type PKUNZIP followed by the name of the compressed file. You probably want to create a new directory in which to do this, to prevent a possibly large number of separate files from cluttering up an existing directory.

- Once your component files are unloaded and in working order, you can delete the original compressed file. You don't need it anymore.

There are a few other file types you might encounter which require decompression. The good news is that the two utilities mentioned above will decompress these files as well! So the above steps apply, except that you substitute the appropriate file extension for ".ZIP" or ".sit".

Utility...	*...will also decompress*
WinZip	.GZ, .LHZ, .ARJ, .ARC, .TAR, .TGZ, .TAZ, .Z
StuffIt Expander	.gz, .zip, .arj, .arc, .bin, .hqx

Sometimes one or more files have been bundled together and compressed into a "self-extracting archive." This simply means that the file you obtain is executable, and that when you run/launch it, it will decompress itself. On Windows machines, these files have extensions of ".EXE"; on Macs, they usually have extensions of ".sea."

CHAPTER 6

Creating a Genealogy Home Page

I F YOU'VE BEEN FORTUNATE ENOUGH TO COME ACROSS A PRINTED GENEALOGY THAT CHRONICLES ONE OF YOUR FAMILY LINES, you know what a valuable reference it can be. But you also know what a trial it can be to track the generations across multiple chapters—and that's when the book is *well* written, organized, and indexed. Part of the problem is that a family tree is a three-dimensional structure, with many twisting and overlapping branches, and the writer's job is to press that delicate design into a *two*-dimensional form on the printed page.

Well, the hypertext publishing that you've been perusing on the Web is a new form of publishing that finally lets you write in *three* dimensions. You can connect people, documents, and events to each other in ways that make sense to you—not to the confines of the printed page.

Even if you have no interest in placing your genealogy on the Web for the public to see, you might want to consider creating a hypertext document to store and display your family history. In this chapter, you'll learn:

- *About HTML—and why you need it*
- *How to create an HTML document*
- *How to use graphics efficiently*

What Is HTML—And Why Do I Need It?

HTML, Hypertext Markup Language, is one of the two popular formats people use to put their genealogies on the Web. (The other, GEDCOM, is discussed in chapter 4.) All of those documents you've seen on the Web—with flashy embedded graphics and hyperlinks laced throughout—were created using HTML.

Many people in the publishing industry are getting excited about HTML for good reason: It could cause as dramatic a revolution in publishing as Gutenberg's printing press caused in the 1400s. Because readers can follow any trail of hyperlinks they wish, no two readers will have the same experience with a publication. And, in a sense, the reader is not just passively reading the document, but rather *interacting* with it. The reader is in effect asking the document, "Show me this. Ok, now show me *this*."

HTML offers new possibilities for published genealogies, too. (See "Publishing on the Leading Edge," page 85.) Imagine reading a page that contains information on a family; to follow the line of one child, you just click on that child's name and you're there. No thumbing back to the index and then tracking down each of the twenty "John Allens" in order to figure out which is the right one. Imagine paging through a series of wills to track the successive partitioning that pared down your family's original farm. Imagine clicking on an icon to view a photo gallery, a copy of grandmother's wedding announcement, or a page from the family Bible with your great-great-grandfather's handwriting, recording the births of his sons and daughters.

Sound exciting? It is. But before you proceed, keep in mind the one major drawback of HTML: it's not a database. While updating an HTML document is as easy as editing a letter saved in a word processor, HTML won't give you the database search functions (show me a list of all people who lived in Milwaukee between 1800 and 1850) you need to keep serious research up to date. And HTML won't let you export your data in GEDCOM, which you need to participate in online genealogy repositories. You may find yourself trying to update two documents at once: your database program and your HTML document. You'll be

PUBLISHING ON
THE LEADING EDGE

eb-based publishing is still in its infancy, and one of the hurdles traditional publishers are still working out is how they are still going to make money publishing on the Web, where access to all material has traditionally been free of charge. Only in 1996 did publications as diverse as Penthouse *and* The Wall Street Journal *begin charging subscription fees for access to their sites, and it's still too soon to tell how well they'll fare. But people don't publish their genealogies to make money; they publish to preserve their work for their cousins and descendants for posterity. Right?* Right?

doing twice the work, and it won't be long before your two sets of data will be out of sync.

How to Create an HTML Document

Perhaps you should consider creating an HTML record of your history to be an "end stage" project, much like writing a book would be. Although genealogy is never "finished," at some point you have to stop and say, "Here is my family history. Let's publish it." But when you are ready to take the plunge, here are the three major routes to producing an HTML document:

❧ **Use *GED2HTML*,** a software package written by Gene Stark that will automatically convert genealogical databases into HTML. *GED2HTML* is firmly established in the market, but commercial database packages are now offering similar, automated HTML generation features. One such package is "Family Gathering" by Palladium Interactive.

To use *GED2HTML*, you simply export a GEDCOM file from your database, execute *GED2HTML*, and specify the name of the GEDCOM file you wish to convert. If you don't change the default settings, *GED2HTML* will generate an HTML file like this one:

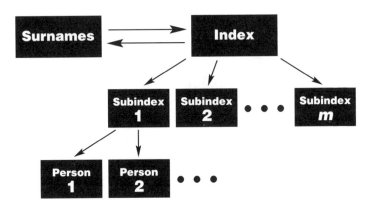

Figure 6-1. Default *GED2HTML* Tree Structure

Some of the changes you can make include the number of lines placed in each index file, which adjusts the rate at which the tree's branches expand; individuals per file; files per directory; and pedigree depth. For more information on *GED2HTML*, see Gene Stark's home page at http://www.gendex.com/ged2html/.

Advantages: It's easy. You don't have to make any of the HTML design decisions yourself; you just run the program and the document is automatically generated. Also, you don't need to keep two separate programs up-to-date. If you update your database, you just rerun *GED2HTML* and—viola!—you have a whole new HTML document, too.

Disadvantages: If you want your home page to look different than the template the utility program uses to generate HTML, you may be out of luck. Although there is some flexibility in how HTML is generated, making fundamental changes in how your page is to be structured is difficult. Also, if you want to incorporate graphics, special fonts, or forms (such as a search engine), you will have to add these manually.

🔁 **Start from scratch.** (Don't cringe and leave just yet!) HTML is not a programming language like FORTRAN; it's a markup language. A "markup language" is a language in which ordinary text is interspersed with special commands, called tags, which indicate how the text functions in the doc-

A WORD ABOUT COPYRIGHTS

One of the new issues that Web publishing raises is copyright infringement. Once anything—an article, a picture, a simple graphic—appears on the Internet, it is simple for anyone with Web access to copy it onto his or her home computer. However, you must be very careful before you use any of this seemingly free information on your own public Web page.

According to Cyberspace and the Law, *by Cavazos and Morin,* any material placed on the Internet—even if it's placed in a public forum, such as a news group—carries with it the original author's copyright. Technically speaking, any redistribution of the information—even something as innocent as re-posting an article to a different news group—constitutes a violation of the copyright. This goes against our intuition. After all, we might ask, "Why would the author post the message if he didn't want it to be widely read?" But one can imagine a situation in which an author may wish to be associated with

certain news groups and not others; or with some publications and not others. Someone running for public office would not want his words taken out of context in a tabloid article announcing the spotting of Elvis!

This doesn't mean that you can never use any material posted by someone else. It simply means that you must obtain permission before you do so. In general, people are willing and eager to have their words or images seen by the widest possible audience. Many people enjoy designing unique and colorful buttons, bars, and other images, and they will offer a selection on the Web that are free for the taking. Always look for a copyright notice, but remember that these people want you to use their images; they offer them in part to see how many people will take them. Some will ask that, if you use the image on a public page, you include a credit to the artist.

Remember—it's not just a common courtesy— it's the law!

ument. Remember the original word processors? In addition to letters and punctuation, you had to type in special characters that showed where you wanted to insert italics, bold, new fonts, and other commands, and you also had to type in characters to show where you wanted those characteristics to end.

That's exactly how HTML works, too. As an example, here's how HTML is used to italicize the word *ancestor:* <i>ancestor.</i> In HTML, a code enclosed in these brackets < > starts a new characteristic, and the same code after a slash ends it. Most HTML codes occur in pairs—one to start and one to stop the formatting. Here are a few common tag pairs:

<b> this text will appear in boldface </b>
<em> this text is emphasized </em>
<strong> this is more strongly emphasized </strong>

Likewise, to tell the computer where you want to insert a graphic, you type a special command <img src="family.jpg"> in the spot where you want an image to appear. When the browser encounters that command, it will go and look for the graphics file named "family.jpg" that you stored in the same

CREATING A SIMPLE HTML DOCUMENT

Let's run through a step-by-step tour to creating a simple HTML document. For our purposes, let's assume that you are not using one of the Web authoring tools or a "what-you-see-is-what-you-get" (WYSIWYG) word processor which automatically generates the hypertext markup tags for you. You might be using an older word processor, or simply a text editor.

■ If you're using an old-style word processor, make sure that it will save documents in ASCII, which is a common format readable to all types of Web browsers. Look for an ASCII option under the "Save As . . ." menu option.

■ Create a document called "trial.htm" or "trial.html." (It is best to give HTML documents names ending in these suffixes, since some Web browsers look for this.)

■ Type the following exactly:
　　<html>
　　<body>
　　I made this!
　　</body>
　　</html>

■ Save the file in ASCII format.

directory as your HTML file. Even the hyperlinks are that simple. Suppose you wanted to send the reader to the Web site www.sherlockholmes.com/ when he clicks on the word "elementary." The command would look like this:

<a href=http://www.sherlockholmes.com/> elementary </a>

The only part of this that the reader will see on his screen is the word "elementary," which will appear highlighted and underscored to show that it's a link. (See "Creating a Simple HTML Document," opposite.)

Advantages: Creating your document from scratch means that you have maximum ability to design your genealogy any way you want. You can show off your family coat-of-arms, you can cross-reference the texts of wills, marriage certificates and deeds, you can link to historical essays that add a backdrop

- ➤

■ *Open your Web browser. From the pull-down menu under "FILE," select "Open Local Document," and in the window find and click on "trial.htm." You should see "I made this!"*

■ *Go back to your word processor and create a second document called "link.htm" or "link.html." In it, type the following:*
> *<html>*
> *<body>*
When I click on the words below, I will see my trial document:
<a href="trial.htm">GO NOW!</a>
> *</body>*
> *</html>*

■ *Save the document (again, in ASCII) in the same directory or folder, and go back to your Web*

browser. Choose "Open Local Document" again and open "link.htm."

■ *CLICK ON YOUR HYPERLINK!*

The <html> and <body> commands tell your browser where the document begins and ends. A more thorough lesson in HTML is beyond the scope of this book, but there are several ways to learn more:

■ **Browse online tutorials**
There are a number of good documents about HTML right on the Web. Two good ones are A Beginner's Guide to HTML by the National Center for Supercomputing Applications (http://www.ncsa.uiuc.edu/General/ Internet/WWW/HTMLPrimer.html)

and Spinning the Web: An Introduction to HTML *by James Powell of the Virginia Polytechnic Institute and State University (http://scholar.lib.vt.edu/reports/soasis-slides/HTML-Intro.html).*

■ **Buy a book on HTML**
Bookstores and computer stores are filled with books on HTML publishing. Here are just a couple of examples:

—Teach Yourself Web Publishing with HTML in 14 Days *by Laura Lemay (Sams.net Publishing)*

—Foundations of World Wide Web Programming with HTML & CGI *by Tittle, Gaither, Hassinger, and Erwin (IDG Books Worldwide, Inc.)*

■ **Check your sources**
The pull-down menu under "File" on your browser will also give you an option called "Document source." If you're surfing on the Web, and you come across a page that you especially like, click on "Document Source." You'll see the markup tags the writer used to create the page. While you shouldn't just copy someone else's work, you may learn some tricks and techniques to make your own page more appealing. (See "A Word About Copyrights," page 87.)

---

to your heritage, you can link each person to their bibliographic references, and you can stretch to the limits of your imagination. Plus, you don't have to acquire any special software. All you need is a word processor capable of exporting files in ASCII, which most can do today, and an ordinary Web browser.

Disadvantages: You lose your database search-and-retrieval functions. Once the page is designed, it's stuck in that format until you change it. In other words, you can't just click a few buttons and generate a new type of tree, the way you can with database programs. To include a tree in your HTML document, you'd have to type in all of the hypertext tags one at a time, and then retype them each time there was a change. In addition, you will need to learn the syntax of the HTML tags. As you enhance your Web page to make it more appealing, your knowledge of HTML must expand accordingly.

WRITING FROM SCRATCH

Here's an example of a genealogical page written from scratch. The page incorporates a small portrait of its subject, and a short summary of vital statistics appears under his name. Hyperlinks connect to similar pages for his parents, his wife, and the son who happens to

Charles Palmer

Born September 16, 1811, in Concord, Pennsylvania. Married March 12, 1833, to Deborah Pitman. Died April 12, 1876. Charles Palmer is the son of John Palmer and Beulah Walter.

On March 12, 1833, he was married to Deborah Pitman by Mayor John Swift of Philadelphia. Their children were Mary F. Palmer *(October 18, 1835 to November 21, 1909)*Lewis Palmer *(October 2, 1837 to ??),* James Palmer *(November 9, 1839 to December 5, 1839)* Edwin H. Palmer *(February 24, 1841 to October 22, 1863),* and Hannah Ann Palmer *March 3, 1843 to March 20, 1843).*[1]

Marriage Will

Mary TUGGLE

- ◌ *BIRTH:* 1790 [S6]
- ◌ *DEATH:* 1857 [S5]
- ◌ *BURIAL:* Patrick Co., VA [S5]

*Father:*Joshua TUGGLE
*Mother:*Elizabeth PACE
Family 1: Prior PENDLETON

- ◌ *MARRIAGE:* 7 SEP 1807, Patrick Co., VA

1. Elizabeth PENDLETON

```
                      John TUGGLE
    Joshua TUGGLE    |
|                     | Mary HOUCHINS
|
|--Mary TUGGLE
|
|                     John PACE
| Elizabeth PACE     |
                     | Susannah HOUCHINS
```

(Above) A manually edited genealogy page

(Left) An automatically generated genealogy page

be in this genealogist's direct line. Icons at the bottom of the screen connect to the text of his will.

By contrast, at left is a page that was automatically generated using the GED2HTML tool.

In the manually edited page, the author was able to include custom icons and other graphics alongside the biographical text. But producing the *document was labor-intensive and will require time-consuming edits every time the author receives new information on this ancestor.*

With the automatically generated page, changes can be made quite easily just by rerunning the utility program (in this case, GED2HTML). But the page doesn't contain any graphical images. This doesn't mean that if you go the automated route you can't have any graphics in your document, or that you can't have other customized features. It just means that you should

separate those pages (files) in your document that you edit by hand from those that you generate through an automated tool.

Also, note that "customization" does not necessarily mean "editing manually." The GED2HTML *utility gives you some flexibility in the overall layout of your genealogy. But if you want to be able to click on an image of your Great Uncle Seth and have him speak to you (by playing a .WAV audio file), you will be doing this manually.*

🐌 **Use an HTML editor,** also called a Web-authoring tool, which is a software package that helps automate some of the process of creating a Web document. Remember the analogy comparing HTML to the older word processors? Newer word processors allow you to simply highlight and click when you want to italicize, for example. (But the tags are still there! The software just hides them from your view!) Likewise, HTML editors automate some of the task of typing in all those tags by hand.

For example, if you click on a button marked "link," the editor brings up a window into which you can type the URL you wish to link to. The program automatically inserts the HTML: <a href=whatever.url.you.entered></a>. While this may not look like a lot to type by hand, it can add up if you are creating a large document or if you frequently edit an existing document. (And it'll save you from those maddening typos!)

A readily available HTML editor is Netscape's *Composer,* which comes with the *Communicator* package. *Composer* displays your Web page almost exactly as it appears in your browser. It's very easy to change the properties of the text, the screen, and other hypertext components, such as tables. You

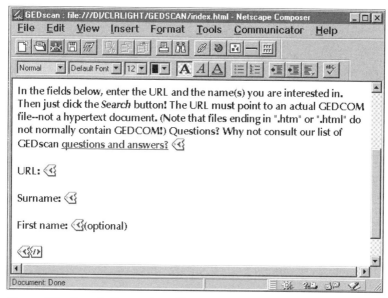

Figure 6-2. Sample Screen from Netscape's *Composer*

can insert, move and delete graphical images in an intuitive way. This certainly beats typing in all those markup tags!

Other HTML editors are available on the Web as shareware. The TUCOWS collection at http://www.sasknet.com/~tucows/ has a nice assortment of such editors. You can also buy commercial HTML editors, such as *HotDog*, developed by Sausage Software (http://www.sausage.com) and published in North America by Anawave Software, Inc. (http://www.anawave.com); and *HTMLed* by Internet Software Technologies (http://www.eucanect.com/software/htmlinfo.html). A sample screen from *HotDog Pro* is shown in figure 6-3. The smaller window in figure 6-3 shows *HotDog*'s "real-time output" feature, which shows you what a portion of your finished Web page will look like, even as you continue to edit the source!

Advantages and Disadvantages: An editor simply makes it easier to design an HTML document; the final product

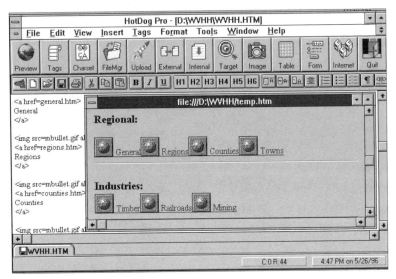

Figure 6-3. Sample Screen from *HotDog Pro*
Used by permission.

would look identical to one you created by typing the codes manually, so the pros and cons would be identical to those listed above.

🐾 **Use a "hypertext-aware" word processor.** Recent versions of popular word processors such as *Microsoft Word* and *WordPerfect* know HTML and will allow you to make changes to your hypertext document in a "what-you-see-is-what-you-get" (WYSIWYG) manner. So if you're updating your home page using *Word* and you click on a "mailto:" link, *Word* will bring up your local e-mail software to send a message. If you click on a link which points to a server on the Web, *Word* will attempt to contact that host and make the connection. Even fill-in forms appear on the screen in nearly the same way they appear in your browser. You may find, however, that these newer word processors are so laden with features that they take a long time to execute their functions. If this is the case, you might be better off using one of the Web-authoring tools of the type mentioned above. Because they have fewer features, they are typically more responsive.

KEEPING YOUR
ITALICS STRAIGHT!

These days, with the rapidly expanding features of word processors such as Microsoft Word and WordPerfect, it is important to keep in mind how hypertext documents are stored. Despite the friendly "what-you-see-is-what-you-get" (WYSIWYG) interfaces, the underlying hypertext document is ultimately saved in simple ASCII. When you instruct your Web browser to show you a particular document, it will expect the file you load to contain only ASCII characters. This ASCII file will contain tags that instruct your browser to display italics, boldface, and headers. It will probably also contain references to other files containing graphics, and may even contain references to executable programs such as CGI scripts (see the glossary) or Java programs.

Why should you be concerned with any of this? You need to make sure that you distinguish between functions that are provided by your word processor and those that are provided by your Web browser. For example, if you create an italicized phrase but fail to save the document in a hypertext format, the italics will have meaning only to your word processor. A document saved in a product-specific format (such as a Microsoft Word document having a file extension of ".DOC") will not be readable by a Web browser. You need to do one of two things: (1) save the document as hypertext (if that option is available), or (2) edit the HTML tags manually and save the file as ASCII.

Another option is to use a text editor. Text editors give you some of the conveniences of word processors, such as word wrap, tabs, cut/paste, and find/replace, but they don't have the fancy design options that aren't strictly necessary to write ASCII documents. So text editors are typically easier to learn and use, smaller (on disk and in memory), and execute more quickly. If you have a PC running MS-Windows, check out Editeur by Jean-Pierre Menicucci at http://www.shareware.com/. If you are using a Mac, try BBEdit by Bare Bones Software at http://www.barebones.com/bbedit.html.

On the other hand, if you already have a word processor that you're comfortable with, there's no reason to go out and get a text editor instead. Just make sure to keep your italics straight!

Use a combined approach. Perhaps the best way to create an online genealogy is to use a combined approach in which you generate some pages within the document automatically and others by hand. Then, when you update your database, you need to replace only those pages that are automatically generated by your conversion utility, and you won't overwrite any changes that you may have made to the other pages.

For example, suppose that you wanted to include a "photo gallery" in your genealogy. You could create a manual home page that would include two links: one to the automatically generated index of surnames and one to the photo gallery. The overall "tree structure" of such a genealogy might look something like:

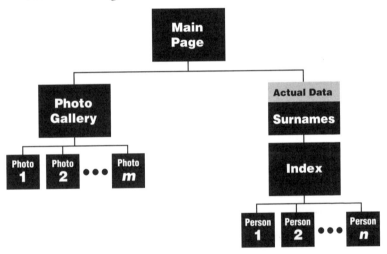

Figure 6-4. Multi-Level HTML Genealogy

The Main Page at the top of the tree is analogous to the cover of a book; you want it to be attractive, enticing the reader to come further. You might include a graphical image of your family's coat of arms or maybe an old group photo of your ancestors—even a photograph of a beautiful tree. When you convert your GEDCOM file into HTML using software, the resulting HTML files replace only the part of the chart marked "ACTUAL DATA" and the boxes below it.

This way, you have the flexibility of creating an alluring Web page that has exactly the structure you want with the convenience of automatic updates to the portions containing actual data.

Tips on Using Graphics

Remember when desktop publishing programs first came out? Suddenly people could quickly and easily use all kinds of outlandish fonts and graphics at the click of a button. And some people went wild; they produced newsletters and memos loaded with so many different fonts and pictures that they were impossible to read!

One of the big advantages of using HTML is the ability to embed graphics into your document quickly and easily. But that doesn't mean you should cram in as many huge pictures as you can! By now in your Web wanderings you've undoubtedly run across pages that were so laden with graphics that they took forever to load, and when you did get to see them, you wondered why you bothered to wait. Well, there are ways to incorporate enough images to keep your screens lively and exciting without overloading readers' patience.

The basic rule of thumb is that the more different images you have, the longer it will take for them all to load. Also, the bigger an image is—that is, the more storage space it takes—the longer it will take for the image to download through a modem, and the more annoyed your readers will get waiting for your document to appear.

⚛ **Scan in gray scale,** especially when using black and white photos. Computers display everything in colored dots called picture elements, or *pixels*. When you scan in color, each pixel must be described by three different numbers to convey that single pixel's intensity in red, green, and blue light. A grey scale image requires only a single number per pixel to describe the intensity (because all shades of gray have equal amounts of red, green, and blue components). So it takes (very roughly) three times as much memory to store a color image as a gray scale image.

⚛ **Keep the resolution low.** Scanners are made for a wide

variety of uses, included sophisticated publishing programs. But images that are ultimately going to end up on the printed page require much higher resolution, or pixel density, than images that are only going to be viewed on a computer screen. Professional publications often use resolutions of 900 or more dpi, or dots per inch. Typical home laser printers print images at a resolution of 300 or 600 dpi. By contrast, even top-of-the-line consumer computer monitors can only display images in a range of up to 100 dpi. So if you scan an image at 600 dpi and then try to display it at 100 dpi, the image will appear much bigger than the physical screen, and you'll have to scroll sideways to even see it all.

Choose the right format. When you scan your photograph, you will be given an option as to which type of graphics file to create, and you'll have many to choose from, each having a different file extension, such as .BMP, .JPG, .GIF, .TIF, etc. The two most widely used graphics formats you will encounter on the Web are GIF (pronounced "jiff" as in "jiffy") and JPEG (pronounced "jay-peg" and having an associated file extension of .JPG). GIF format is more widely used for small, "in-line" graphical images, such as buttons and bars, while JPEG is used more widely for larger images. JPEG format is used for larger

BEYOND HELPER APPLICATIONS: PLUG-INS, JAVA, AND ACTIVE-X

*A*s you've already seen, you can tell your Web browser about helper applications that it can use to display or otherwise format types of data that the browser does not know about inherently. This may include audio samples, certain graphics formats, and compressed or encoded data. The problem with a helper application is that it was probably developed by a different company and probably has a different user interface than your

images because it is usually more compact, so .JPG files are smaller than their corresponding .GIF counterparts.

🌀 **"Hide" your big pictures.** Why not leave it up the reader to decide whether he or she wants to see your biggest and best pictures? Instead of having them open automatically—and slowly—as soon as someone enters your Web page, keep them hidden until the reader asks—with a click—to see them. A good technique that many Web authors use is to present a small image (maybe only one inch square) of a photo in .GIF format. A reader who wishes to view a larger version of the image can click on the small image, which will cause the larger JPEG version to appear. The small .GIF image can be thought of as an icon, as you would find on your Windows or Mac desktop.

🌀 **Re-use images.** An image only has to download once. So if, for example, you'd like to use brightly colored buttons on your page, choose one design and stick to it. Once it downloads, it will appear everywhere, and the reader won't have to sit through ten more downloads.

🌀 **Keep your total number of graphics down.** A few carefully-chosen images which are small- to medium-size will produce a Web page that is both compelling and easy to browse.

--➤

Web browser. The buttons or icons are probably dissimilar, and the helper application will probably appear in a window separate from your browser.

The transition to a helper application has been made more seamless by the "plug-in." A plug-in is a program that is specifically intended to be used in connection with a Web browser. When data requiring a plug-in is loaded, the plug-in takes over, but in such a way that it seems to be a part of the browser itself. Thus, the user can see or hear new types of data without ever leaving the convenience of his or her browser. For example, the Adobe Acrobat Plug-in *allows you to display Acrobat PDF (Portable Document Format) files; the* RealAudio *plug-in allows for the playing of real-time audio clips.*

One problem with plug-ins is that new data formats are constantly being devised to convey graphics, sound, video, and other multimedia information. Suppose you install a plug-in to display (fictitious) Kool-Grafix 2.0 data files, but find out six months later that your plug-in won't display the new KoolGrafix 3.0 format. Clearly, the industry is changing so quickly that even the key players within the industry itself face a great challenge just to keep up with it!

A partial solution to this problem comes with the development of Java applets and Active-X controls. Java is a programming language that (among other things) allows a Web page designer to tell a browser not only what data to display, but how to display it. Microsoft's Active-X provides a similar function, but with a greater emphasis

on Microsoft's operating systems. In Java, a very small program called an "applet" is transmitted with the data. As with a plug-in, an applet allows a browser to represent data types that it ordinarily couldn't. But unlike a plug-in, an applet does not need to be separately purchased or installed. And since applets accompany the data itself, anyone wishing to invent a new data format simply needs to provide a new applet to process it. All of these exchanges between Web site and browser are totally transparent to the user. Thus, a browser that knows about the Java language (that is, is "Java-aware") can theoretically display any type of data that anyone will ever create!

Practice!

Once you start getting the basics down, you'll be able to create a rich assortment of HTML documents using a variety of tools. And you can play and experiment all you want without incurring Internet charges. You don't have to put your family history out on the Web in order to have fun playing with HTML. But if you are considering publishing your work on the Web, you should read chapter 7, especially "Writing Hints," before you get in too deep and find that you have to do a lot of rewriting.

You have the newest publishing tool in the world at your disposal. See what you can do with it!

Publishing Your Site on the Web

A re you ready to take the plunge? The Internet thrives on the willingness of its users to share data. And you're likely to find thousands of genealogists interested in the work you've done.

Once you've created a document that could reside on the Web—GEDCOM or HTML—you have only a few more steps to take to put it out where other people can see it.

In this chapter, you'll learn:

    The easiest route to publishing on the Web

    How to select an ISP for your Web space

    How to use FTP

    How to announce your presence on the Web

The Easiest Way to Publish on the Web

If you want to offer your genealogy on the Web with the smallest possible effort and expense, and you don't want to get "fancy," you can submit your data files to one of the existing online databases or Web pages. Many of the genealogy-related Web pages allow you to submit your genealogy in GEDCOM or HTML form, which they place on their server for you, free of charge.

The disadvantage is that you have no direct access to your genealogy after you give it to them. If you need to make an update, you can't make it yourself. This would include any cosmetic changes (such as new graphics) as well as even basic changes, such as the addition of a new person or life event. If you anticipate a lot of updates, having to go through a Web page owner may get tiresome very quickly for both you and the owner. At a minimum, you will probably want to save a fair number of changes and update your page only occasionally. To see an example of a page where people submit their own genealogies, look at the page for Traveller Southern Families at http://www.traveller.com/genealogy/.

While this approach offers few obstacles to publishing your family history on the Web, it doesn't afford the kind of flexibility that most Web authors prefer. You might want to consider renting your own Web space. If you choose that route, you can use a combination of manual and automated HTML to update your documents at your convenience. Your page will always be up to date and will include the options you choose.

Selecting an ISP for Your Web space

In chapter 2 we discussed how to select an Internet Service Provider (ISP) for your Internet access. Now you face another decision: you must select a provider for your Web space. (See "Why Can't I Turn My Own Computer Into a Web Server?," opposite.) Some ISPs rent storage space on their Web servers to individuals. There, you can store your HTML documents, and anyone who types in that server's URL can view your document. (Your service provider is "renting" only the right to dial in and use its communications lines as well as its mail server.)

The provider you choose for your Web space may be different than the one you select to provide your Internet access. Most companies do offer "package deals" to give you both types of service for a fixed monthly rate, so your first step might by to ask your ISP whether it rents Web space.

However, the best company to provide you with your "on ramp" to the information superhighway isn't always the best place to go for Web space. Some companies have very reasonable rates for leasing their communication lines, but very high rates for setting up Web pages, and vice versa.

There are even some organizations that offer "free" Web space. One popular such organization is Geocities. It offers free Web space to folks who have access to the Web. You may locate your Web page in any of several "neighborhoods," depending on your area of interest. Neighborhoods are set up for enthusiasts in science and technology, arts, politics, and many other areas. The neighborhood "Heartland" contains numerous pages relating to genealogy (among other things). To see a list of these, search for

WHY CAN'T I TURN MY OWN COMPUTER INTO A WEB SERVER?

It's a natural question to ask, but there are several reasons why a typical home computer is just not equipped to be a Web server. A Web server must:

■ *Stay on (nearly) all the time. The Internet never shuts down; its host machines are humming around the clock, except for periodic down time for backups, maintenance, etc.*

■ *Have a static IP address. A client machine (like the one you have at home) knows where to find a server on the Web by the server's IP (Internet Protocol) address. For this reason, a Web server must have an address that never changes—one that is static. The problem facing*

telecommunications today is that the number of available IP addresses is running low. This is partly the reason why your machine is temporarily assigned a dynamic IP address when you dial into your ISP—an address that is good only for the duration of your session. Unless you plan to run an ISP yourself, it may not be cost-effective to obtain a static IP address.

■ *Keep its communication lines open. Teenagers are amateurs compared to the amount of phone (or other type of connect) time a Web server logs. You'd have to have lines that were connected continuously, twenty-four hours a day, seven days a week.*

"genealogy" on the Heartland search screen. You can find Geo-cities at http://www.geocities.com/.

You also need to base your decision on whether your provider offers the services you need. For the purposes of Web authoring, two services are absolutely essential:

Web space. The monthly rates for renting space on a host machine depend on the amount of space you need. "Personal" Web accounts (as opposed to accounts for businesses) typically include 1, 2, or 5 megabytes of space. Unless you have a very large genealogy or lots of graphical images, 5 megabytes should be plenty of space. The best way to determine how much space you need is to create your entire Web page first on your own computer, where you can see how much space it takes up. (If it's too big, consider trimming down the graphics, as discussed in chapter 6.)

An FTP account. In chapter 3 you learned that the file transfer protocol (FTP) is how you download documents from the Web. FTP is also how you *upload* files from your computer to your Web server. You'll find more on FTP later in this chapter. (Of course, you'll keep a duplicate copy on your own machine so that you can update it.)

Those are your two minimum needs. With these two capabilities, you can create a basic Web page and keep it updated. Accounts that offer just these two features are usually available for less than $20 per month.

If you're more adventurous, you might look for one more feature that makes it easier to maintain your Web page and take advantage of some of the more advanced options of HTML:

A telnet account. Telnet allows you to remotely log in to the Web server and issue commands just as you would on your own machine. Well, perhaps not "just as," since your home machine is probably running Microsoft Windows or Macintosh System 7, and most Web servers use the Unix operating system. If you are familiar with Unix, perhaps from your school or workplace, a telnet account would definitely be worthwhile. If not, you may or may not want to venture into the world of Unix, depending on how daring you feel. When you log in remotely to Unix, you are placed in a Unix shell, where you enter commands on a command line, as opposed to a graphical interface. In this respect Unix is similar to DOS, except that Unix commands are much more numerous, powerful, and (unfortunately) cryptic. For example, in DOS you type "dir" to show a directory; in Unix you type "ls." So unless you want to learn a lot of advanced computing, you might want to forgo telnet.

So why even consider a telnet account? Telnet lets you do more than you can do with FTP. FTP lets you upload and download files to and from a host machine. But what if you wanted to create a new directory in the files already on your server? Some versions of FTP won't let you do this. But with telnet, if you, for example, decided to isolate all your JPEG files in a subdirectory, you could telnet into the host computer and type the Unix command "mkdir photo_gallery," and then, "mv *.jpg photo_gallery" to move all the files ending in ".jpg" into the new directory.

Another reason to consider a telnet account is to take advantage of some of the more advanced capabilities of HTML. For example, you can write and test *CGI scripts.* CGI stands for "Common Gateway Interface"; this is the interface used to get outputs from programs run on the Web server to the browser's machine. In other words, when you're browsing, anytime you fill in an electronic form or run a search engine, you are invoking a computer program that someone created. If you want to include features like that on your Web page, you need CGI scripting to create them.

Writing a CGI script requires that you do some computer programming. The programs run on your host machine when someone's browser invokes them and CGI scripting allows the results to be transferred to their local computer. This type of advanced feature is definitely not required if all you want to do is put your genealogy on the Internet. But if you (or someone you know) is really "into" computer programming, these advanced features might be just the ticket to give your Web page that extra mark of distinction.

Finally, you should keep in mind that many Internet Service Providers will give you free Web space if you open an account having a full range of features. So opening an account that includes a telnet login may provide not only the telnet capability but a home for your Web page as well.

Using FTP

Once you have gotten some Web space, it's time to transfer your files from your home computer onto the server using FTP, which is simply a protocol by which files can be transferred

WRITING HINTS

I n chapter 6 we discussed the mechanics of creating an HTML document. But if you know before you start that you're going to place your documents on the Web, your choice of Web page provider could in part determine how you write and for-mat your own copy of your document on your computer.

■ If you have a telnet account, you can create and edit directories and subdirectories directly on your server. But whatever structure you create there you should also mimic on your home machine (to keep your maintenance under control).

■ Remember the naming conventions for various systems. In chapter 6 we pointed out that your HTML doc-uments could end in either ".htm" or ".html"; the difference is that

some systems, such as Unix machines and Macs, will accept four-character filename extensions, whereas older IBM-compatible systems allow only three characters. Similarly, older IBM-compatible systems will accept only eight characters in the filename.

Also, although the Mac will allow you to use blank spaces in a file name, you should avoid doing so because referring to those files with a Unix shell on your server can be tricky. For example, if you wanted to use the Unix "cat" com-mand to display the contents of the file "my family," you couldn't sim-ply type "cat my family." This command will cause Unix to look for two files—one called "my" and another called "family."

between two computers on the Internet. (See "Why Use FTP?," page 108.) The term "FTP" also refers to the programs used to transfer the files; early versions of such programs were invoked simply by typing the command "FTP." The term is also used as a verb: to FTP a file from your computer to the host.

Depending on what software you have on your PC or Mac, and which Internet service provider you are using, you will have a different "flavor" of FTP. You might have a very friendly, point-and-click interface to FTP; these are discussed later in this chapter. The first type of FTP to appear on the scene used a command-line interface. We'll discuss this one first (briefly), although it has been largely replaced by more friendly, graphical interfaces. Later in the chapter, you'll appreciate the graphical versions even more!

When you activate FTP, one of the first requests you'll see is for the name of a host machine. You should type in the IP address of your host server, which looks like an e-mail address without the "userid@" part. After your computer has connected with the host, you'll see a window into which you can type FTP commands. Your first task is to log in with an FTP login ID and a password.

If you are logging in as "anonymous," (e.g., in order to retrieve a file from a public directory), you will be prompted to provide your full e-mail address as your password. If you are logging in to your own, personal account (for example, to upload your genealogy to your Web server), you will use a login ID and password provided to you by the administrator of the FTP server.

Once you have logged in, the two main commands you will use in FTP are "get" and "put." As you might expect from their names, these commands retrieve data from a host and transfer data to a host, respectively. Here's how they work. (In describing the syntax of these commands here, we use angled brackets < > to indicate strings that you choose, so don't enter the brackets—substitute the actual filenames for the bracketed names.)

The "get" command retrieves the file having a name <host_filename> and places it on your local machine with the

WHY USE FTP?

When you're surfing on the Net with your Web browser, you can click on any type of file you want—FTP, text, GEDCOM, executable, graphics, audio, and compressed files—and download it to your computer without using FTP. So why use FTP? Doesn't the Web browser give you everything you need? Yes and no, for two reasons:

- **Your browser may not allow you to upload.** Netscape Navigator *will allow you to upload a file using anonymous FTP. But if your FTP login is "non-anonymous" (i.e., it requires a password known only to you),* Navigator *does not allow*

uploads (at least as of this writing). For such uploads, you will need an FTP program.

- **FTP is sometimes easier to use.** *Even when you're only downloading, you may still want to use FTP software because some packages are very friendly and are especially designed for navigating complex hierarchical file systems (directories, subdirectories, etc.) If you want to transfer a large number of files, an FTP program might let you do them all with just a few clicks of the mouse, while a browser might make you do each one individually. It's a matter of using the right tool for the right job!*

name <local_filename>:

get <host_filename> <local_filename>

Similarly, the command

put <local_filename> <host_filename>

transfers the file in the opposite direction. For both commands, you can omit the second filename if you don't wish to rename it.

Here are a few other commands you need to know about. Just like your home machine, a host server has a hierarchical structure of directories or folders. When you get or put a file, you must make sure that you are in the proper directory—both at the host end and on your local machine.

dir Shows you a list of all files in the host's current working directory.

pwd Displays the name of the current working directory on the host.

cd Changes the current directory, just as the same command does in DOS (except that Unix machines use forward slashes (/) to delimit directories, rather than the DOS backslash (\). Most versions of FTP use the Unix forward slash, regardless of the type of host machine).

There are "local" versions of the above commands which perform analogous functions on your local machine: ldir, lpwd, and lcd.

The next two commands you need to use require that you understand the difference between the two types of file transfer: ASCII and binary. Files containing text (including HTML documents and GEDCOM files) should be transferred using ASCII mode. If you wish to transfer a file containing graphics, an executable program or compressed data, you will need to transfer it in binary mode. You need to transfer to binary mode before you can upload a binary document.

bin Switches you into binary mode. (When you begin an FTP session, you are automatically in ASCII mode.)

asc Switches you back into ASCII mode.

But this FTP command may be the most important:

quit Ends an your FTP session. (Sometimes software documentation tells you exactly how to start a program, but doesn't bother to tell you how to stop it!)

These are the most basic and useful FTP commands, but there are dozens more. If you're curious, type "?" at the FTP prompt to display a list of commands. Typing "help" followed by the name of a particular command will get a short description.

Point-and-Click

After you log in to some FTP software, instead of a command-line box, you will see two windows which look somewhat like *Windows Explorer*; they show directory hierarchies. One window shows the file system on the host; the other, on your local computer. You can use this program just as you would *Windows Explorer*. You can drag files from any directory and drop them into any other. You can also perform other file management functions, such as deleting a file—regardless of where the file is located. You can even create a new directory on the host system (something you can't normally do with the old, character-based FTP). Here is what this command interface looks like with Spry Inc.'s *Network File Manager:*

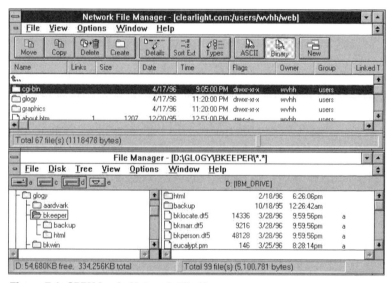

Figure 7-1. SPRY Inc.'s *Network File Manager*
SPRY is the Internet division of CompuServe. Used by permission. All rights reserved.

If you are familiar with *File Manager* in Windows 3.1 or *Windows Explorer* in Windows 95, this program gives you an easier way to transfer files. The fact that some of the file systems are local and

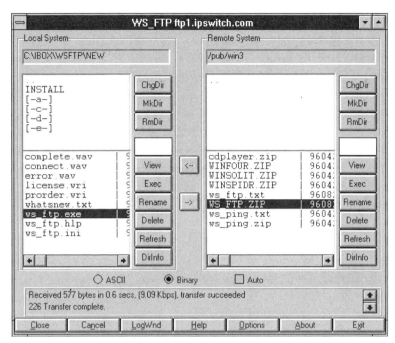

Figure 7-2. John A. Junod's *WS-FTP* Program
Used by permission.

others remote is totally transparent to you. The only thing that might "give away" this fact is the use of differing file naming conventions in the various operating systems. For example, in Figure 7-1, the top window shows a file system on a Unix machine. The file information is presented in the format used by the Unix "ls" command. But with this small, cosmetic difference, *Network File Manager* works just like Windows *File Manager*. And you don't need to type in any of those commands, such as cd, pwd, or bin.

Perhaps an even easier FTP program is one called *FTP Client for Windows (WS-FTP),* written by John A. Junod and copyrighted by Ipswitch, Inc., of Wakefield, Massachusetts. *WS-FTP* brings up a single window having two sides—one side for local files, another for remote files. It works in much the same way as *Network File Manager.* However, having all the files together in a single window makes the program somewhat easier to use. One especially nice feature of *WS-FTP* is that it will automatically try to figure out whether a given file should be transferred in ASCII or binary mode. So unless you are transferring some really strange files, *WS-FTP* lets you forget about this detail. If you need to override the choice *WS-FTP* makes, a mouse click can force the program into ASCII or binary mode. *WS-FTP* is not shareware; it may be used free of charge by individuals for home, non-commercial use. You can find it at http://204.71.8.24/JUNODJ/.

If you are using a Macintosh, you could use Dartmouth's program Fetch. The program features the standard, friendly graphical interface that made the Mac famous:

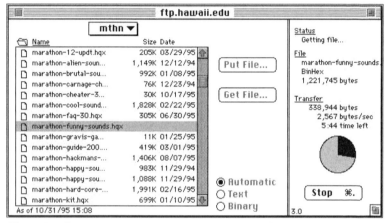

Figure 7-3. Dartmouth's *Fetch* Program for the Macintosh
Used by permission.

When you launch *Fetch,* you are shown the file system of the remote host in the same format the Mac uses for its own folder structure. You can then click on "get" and "put" buttons, or you can retrieve a file by double-clicking on it. As with *WS-FTP,* you can ask *Fetch* to determine the appropriate file transfer mode. To find out more about *Fetch,* see Dartmouth's Web page at http://www.dartmouth.edu/pages/softdev/fetch.html.

Announcing Your Presence

Once your document is safely ensconced in its Web home and everything is up and running, you have one more step to take: Let everyone know you're there!

We mentioned that the search engines that help people hunt

the Web won't turn up a particular site unless its been told that the file exists. If you want the engines to show your file, you have to inform them that your site is ready and waiting for visitors.

For AltaVista, Yahoo!, and WebCrawler, you can perform this function automatically by clicking on the "Add URL" button and entering your own URL. Or, rather than go to all of them manually, some people on the Web have made your task a little easier. (Imagine that!) For example, go to *Submit It!* at http://www.submit- it.com/. Here, you can fill in a form specifying what your site is about, and which search engines you want to notify, and Submit It! will notify all of them automatically.

WATCH YOUR STEP!

Once your work is on its Web server, people all over the world can see what you wrote. And while this powerful new capability can dramatically improve the achievements of genealogy, it can also amplify the problems.

If you put incorrect information on the Internet, it may be difficult to retract your error! You can change it as soon as you know of the error, but you have no way of knowing how many people may have seen the information and copied it, not knowing of the mistake. Of course, this sort of problem existed before the Internet did, but because it takes so much longer to disseminate information in books, the damage was more limited. On the other hand, you can't correct a hardcopy book as quickly as an electronic document, so the error exists longer!

Here are some tips to make sure that your work does not violate the integrity of databases the world over:

■ **Verify! Verify! Verify!** *While you're creating your Web page on your home computer, triple check the facts before you upload onto your server.*

■ **Document!** *You've already learned that you need to verify your sources before you accept someone else's work into your own genealogy. Be sure to show your own sources, too.*

■ **Label!** *If any of your information is at all speculative or represents contradictions, be sure to label the questionable material clearly. If an individual has two different birth dates from two different sources, label both dates and both sources.*

In addition to the search engines, you might also want to inform the owners of other Web pages related to yours. For example, if your genealogy is predominantly Jewish or African-American or Norwegian, and you know of a page that is gathering a compendium of Web-based resources in those areas, you should send an e-mail note to the owners of the compendium. Maybe they'll build links to your page! (Maybe you could reciprocate by adding links to their pages from yours!) Similarly, you probably want to post messages to related newsgroups.

That sort of mutual linking is how much of the interlacing of documents on the Web begins and grows. It won't be long before your page is tied into a large community of genealogists that is dedicated to building and preserving our heritage in a collective "library."

You've joined a new world. The globe is at your fingertips, you've visited libraries you've never seen, and you've met people you'll never talk to. They've given you a universe of resources, and you're giving back all you can, too. This new world you're helping to create is still in its infancy, but it is growing stronger and faster each time a new person joins.

Welcome to the twenty-first century.

Bibliography

Cavazos, Edward A., and Gavino Morin. *Cyberspace and the Law.* Massachusetts Institute of Technology, 1994.

Crowe, Elizabeth Powell. *Genealogy Online: Researching Your Roots.* Windcrest/McGraw Hill, 1995.

Dern, Daniel P. *The Internet Guide for New Users.* McGraw-Hill Inc., 1994.

Erwin, Mike, Ed Tittel, Mark Gaither, and Sebastian Hassinger. *Foundations of World Wide Web Programming with HTML and CGI.* Programmer's Press, 1995.

Feudo, Christopher V. *The Computer Virus Desk Reference.* R. R. Donnelley & Sons Co., 1992.

Gaffin, Adam. *The Big Dummy's Guide to the Internet.* Electronic Frontier Foundation, 1993.

Hoffman, Lance J., ed. *Rogue Programs: Viruses, Worms, and Trojan Horses.* Van Nostrand Reinhold, 1990.

James, Phil. *Official Netscape Navigator 2.0 Book.* Netscape Press, 1996.

Krol, Ed. *The Whole Internet User's Guide.* O'Reilly & Associates, 1994.

Lichty, Tom. *The Official America Online For Windows Tour Guide.* Ventana Press, 1993.

Lemay, Laura. *Teach Yourself Web Publishing with HTML in 14 Days.* Sams.net Publishing, 1995.

Morgan, Kenneth O., ed. *The Oxford Illustrated History of Britain.* Oxford University Press, 1984.

Palmer, Laurie. "Getting Started on the Internet." *Journal of the American Health Information Management Association* 66 (8) (September 1995).

Pence, Richard A., ed. *Computer Genealogy: A Guide to Research through High Technology.* Salt Lake City: Ancestry, 1991.

Rheingold, Howard. *The Virtual Community: Homesteading on the Electronic Frontier.* Addison-Wesley, 1993.

Useful Web Pages for Genealogical Research

THIS LIST REPRESENTS JUST THE BEGINNING OF THE GENEAL-OGY-RELATED RESOURCES YOU'LL FIND ON THE WORLD WIDE WEB. While the Web also holds a wealth of material that's geared toward local areas (many county historical societies now have Web pages, for example) and narrow special interests, this index is geared toward more general topics that should be useful to a broader number of people. Start here, though, to find compendium pages with pointers to a vast array of local pages.

The Web is fast becoming a genealogical gold mine. Here are your pickaxe and pan: Good luck!

General

The Genealogy Home Page:
> http://www.genhomepage.com/

Helm's Genealogy Toolbox:
> http://genealogy.tbox.com/genealogy.html

Cyndi's List:
> http://www.oz.net/~cyndihow/sites.htm

A Barrel of Links:
> http://cpcug.org/user/jlacombe/mark.html

Ancestry Home Town:
> http://www.ancestry.com

Genealogy Gateway:
  http://www.polaris.net/~legend/genealogy.htm

Treasure Maps:
  http://www.firstct.com/fv/tmapmenu.html

Everton's Genealogical Helper Online:
  http://www.everton.com/ghonline.html

Genealogy SF:
  http://roxy.sfo.com/~genealogysf/

Cool sites for Genealogists:
  http://www.cogensoc.org/cgs/cgs-cool.htm

Genealogy Online:
  http://genealogy.emcee.com/

Journal of Online Genealogy:
  http://www.onlinegenealogy.com/

GarySC Genealogy:
  http://www.rain.org/~garysc/fmlytree.html

Gene Stark's Genealogy Homepage:
  http://bsd7.cs.sunysb.edu/~stark/genealogy.html

Genealogy Resources on the Internet:
  http://pmgmac.micro.umn.edu/genealogy.html

The Olive Tree:
  http://www.rootsweb.com/~ote/

Genealogy Resources on the Net:
  http://www-personal.umich.edu/~cgaunt/gen_int1.html

WPA Life Histories:
  http://lcweb2.loc.gov/wpaintro/wpahome.html

Genealogies and Online Databases

GENDEX:
  http://www.gendex.com/

GenServ Homepage:
  http://soback.kornet.nm.kr/~cmanis/

GEDCOM Files at Genealogy Online:
  ftp://ftp.genealogy.org/pub/genealogy/GEDCOM

GenWeb Demo:
  http://demo.genweb.org/gene/genedemo.html

Surname Queries/Lists

Genealogy Newsgroups, Mailings Lists:
  http://www.eskimo.com/~chance/

ROOTS-L:
  http://www.smartlink.net/~leverich/roots-l.html

ROOTS-L Gopher:
  gopher://FTP.cac.psu.edu/11/genealogy/roots-l

Roots Surname Finder:
  http://searches.rootsweb.com/cgi-bin/Genea/rsl

Roots Location Finder:
  http://searches.rootsweb.com/cgi-bin/Genea/rll

Genealogy Mail Lists:
  http://users.aol.com/johnf14246/gen_mail.html

United States by Region

New England Historic Genealogical Society:
  http://www.nehgs.org/

Travellers Southern Families:
  http://www.traveller.com/genealogy/

Ohio River Valley Families:
  http://www.trilithic.com/orvf/

The Palatines to America:
  http://genealogy.org/~palam/

Allegheny Regional Family History Society:
http://www.swcp.com/~dhickman/arfhs.html

Cajun Clickers:
http://www.intersurf.com/~cars/

United States, Indexed by State

Cyndi's List: Listing by State:
http://www.oz.net/~cyndihow/usa.htm

Genealogy in the U.S.: Listing by State:
http://www.everton.com/usa.html

African-American

African-American Genealogy for Beginners:
http://www.kdla.state.ky.us/arch/biblforb.htm

African-American History:
http://www.msstate.edu/Archives/History/USA/
Afro-Amer/afro.html

The Afrigeneas Homepage:
http://www.msstate.edu/Archives/History/afrigen/

African Studies:
http://www.sas.upenn.edu/African_Studies/Home_Page/
WWW_Links.html

Latin American

CLNet Research Center:
http://latino.sscnet.ucla.edu/research/

Institute for Genealogy and History for Latin America:
http://www1.infowest.com/homepage/lplatt/

Jewish

JewishGen:
http://www.jewishgen.org/faqinfo.html

Jewish Genealogy Homepage:
  http://129.119.19.103/dvjcc/dvjcc.genealogy.html

Dallas Jewish Genealogy Guide:
  http://129.119.19.103/dvjcc/gwSection2.html

Native-American

NativeWeb:
  http://web.maxwell.syr.edu/nativeweb/

The People's Paths:
  http://www.cris.com/~Nlthomas/paths.html

Oneida Indian Nation:
  http://one-web.org/oneida/

Cherokee National Historical Society:
  http://www.Powersource.com/heritage/

Soft Cherokee Winds:
  http://www2.gamewood.net/cherokee

Yanusdi's Cherokee Heritage Page:
  http://www.public.usit.net/jerercox/

Quaker

Religious Society of Friends:
  http://www.quaker.org/

The Quaker Resources Page:
  http://www.best.com/~reed/quaker.html

Canada

Canadian National Archives:
  http://www.archives.ca/

Acadian Genealogy Home Page:
  http://tdg.uoguelph.ca/~ycyr/genealogy/

Canadian Genealogy:
http://www.FreeNet.Calgary.ab.ca/science/genealogy/cdngene.html

Canadian Immigration:
http://www.archives.ca/www/ImmigrationRecords.html

Search 1871 Census of Canada-Ontario:
http://stauffer.queensu.ca/docsunit/searchc71.html

Eastern Townships—Quebec:
http://www.magicnet.net/~moodies/et2.html

British Columbia Archives and Records Service:
http://www.bcars.gs.gov.bc.ca/bcars.html

United Kingdom and Ireland

UK and Ireland Genealogy:
http://cs6400.mcc.ac.uk/genuki/

A-Z of British Genealogy:
http://midas.ac.uk/genuki/big/EmeryPaper.html

Britain in the U.S.A.:
http://britain.nyc.ny.us/bis/fsheets/3.htm

Irish Family History Foundation:
http://www.mayo-ireland.ie/roots.htm

National Archives of Ireland:
http://www.kst.dit.ie/nat-arch/genealogy.html

IRLGEN: Tracing Your Irish Ancestors:
http://www.bess.tcd.ie/roots_ie.htm

Green Pages: Directory of Irish Sites:
http://www.best.com:80/~paddynet/pages/

Scottish Genealogy Society:
http://www.taynet.co.uk/users/scotgensoc/

Continental Europe

Emigration from Germany:
http://w3g.med.uni-giessen.de/gene/www/emig/emigr.html

Genealogy and History in France:
http://www.wp.com/gefrance/locate.htm

Genealogy in Belgium:
http://win-www.uia.ac.be/u/pavp/genbel.html

Genealogy Benelux Home Page:
http://www.ufsia.ac.be/genealogy/genealog.htm

Flemish Society of Genealogists:
http://win-www.uia.ac.be/u/pavp/vvf.html

Holland Page:
http://ourworld.compuserve.com/homepages/paulvanv/

East European Family History Societies:
http://www.dcn.davis.ca.us/~feefhs/

German-Russian Genealogy:
http://pixel.cs.vt.edu/library/odessa.html

RussLinks:
http://users.aimnet.com/~ksyrah/ekskurs/russlink.html

Ukrainian Genealogy and Heritage:
http://ic.net/~ggressa/ukr.html

Polish Regional Page:
http://www.qrz.com/gene/reg/ESE/poland.html

How to Trace Your Ancestors in Norway:
http://www.norway.org/ancestor.htm

Genealogy in Scandinavia:
http://www.algonet.se/~floyd/scandgen

Swedish Genealogy Page:
http://www.ts.umu.se/~petersj/swegen.html

Asia

Genealogy in Non-Western Civilizations:
  http://win-www.uia.ac.be/u/pavp/ggnwest.html

Reference Documents for Chinese Culture:
  http://acc6.its.brooklyn.cuny.edu/~phalsall/refdocs.html

Legendary/Historical Figures in Japan:
  http://www.io.com/~nishio/japan/figure.html

Australia

Genealogy in Australia:
  http://www.pcug.org.au/~mpahlow/welcome.html

Australian Family History Compendium:
  http://www.cohsoft.com.au/afhc/

Australian Archives:
  http://www.aa.gov.au:80/AA_WWW/AA_Holdings/
  AA_Genie/Genie.html

Immigration

National Archives:
  http://gopher.nara.gov:70/0/genealog/holdings/catalogs/ipcat/
  ipcat.html

Death Records/Cemeteries

Ontario Cemetery Finding Aid:
  http://www.islandnet.com/ocfa/search.html

The Electric Cemetery:
  http://www.ionet.net/~cousin

Association for Gravestone Studies:
  http://www.berkshire.net/ags/

Cemetery Listing Association:
  http://mininet.smu.edu/cla/index.htm

Libraries/Archives

HYTELNET:
   http://library.usask.ca/hytelnet/

Libweb:
   http://sunsite.berkeley.edu/Libweb/

U.S. Library of Congress Search:
   http://lcweb.loc.gov/z3950/mums2.html

LC Reading Room:
   gopher://marvel.loc.gov/11/research/reading.rooms/
   genealogy

American Genealogical Lending Library:
   http://www.agll.com/

Public Access Library Catalogs (dialup and telnet):
   http://www.genealogy.org/~ngs/dialup.html

Archives and Libraries:
   http://www.everton.com/archives.html

U.S. National Archives:
   http://www.nara.gov/

Maps

Maps in Genealogy:
   http://info.er.usgs.gov/fact-sheets/genealogy/index.html

U.S. Geological/Geographical Survey:
   gopher://george.peabody.yale.edu:71/1

Geographic Names Info System:
   http://www-nmd.usgs.gov/www/gnis/gnisform.html

Civil War

U.S. Civil War Center:
   http://www.cwc.lsu.edu

The American Civil War Archives:
   http://www.access.digex.net/~bdboyle/cw.html

Civil War Photographs at the Library of Congress:
   http://rs6.loc.gov/cwphome.html

VMI Archives—Civil War Page:
   http://www.vmi.edu/~archtml/cwsource.html

Civil War General Interest Links:
   http://fly.hiwaay.net/~dsmart/cwlink.html

United States Civil War (1861–1865):
   http://www.cfcsc.dnd.ca/links/milhist/usciv.html

Genealogy and the Civil War:
   http://www.outfitters.com/illinois/history/civil/
   cwgeneal.html

ILTweb: Civil War Home Page:
   http://www.ilt.columbia.edu/k12/history/gb/civilhome.html

American Civil War:
   http://www.historybuff.com/library/refcivil.html

Pictures of the Civil War:
   http://gopher.nara.gov:70/0h/inform/dc/audvis/still/
   civwar.html

American Civil War: Resources on the Internet:
   http://www.dsu.edu/~jankej/civilwar.html

Genealogy Societies

National Genealogical Society:
   http://www.genealogy.org/~ngs/

Federation of Genealogical Societies:
   http://www.fgs.org/~fgs/

U.S. Genealogical and Historical Societies:
   http://www.outfitters.com/genealogy/gensoc/

Daughters of the American Revolution:
http://www.chesapeake.net/DAR

Rand Genealogy Club Home Page:
http://www.rand.org/personal/Genea/

Alberta Genealogical Society:
http://www.terranet.ab.ca/~TurnBL/AGS/AGSMain.html

APG: Salt Lake Chapter:
http://www.gensource.com/APGSLC/

GenTech, Inc.:
http://www.gentech.org/~gentech/

Software Packages

Genealogy Software Springboard
http://www.toltbbs.com/~kbasile/software.html

Brother's Keeper:
http://web.wingsbbs.com/brotherskeepr/

GED2HTML Utility:
http://www.gendex.com/ged2html/

Parsons Technologies (Family Origins):
http://www.parsonstech.com/

Welcome to Family Tree Maker Online:
http://www.familytreemaker.com/

PAF Review Home Page:
http://www.genealogy.org/~paf/

Genealogical Software Archives:
http://www.everton.com/d1.htm

Shareware.com:
http://shareware.com/

Leister Productions (Reunion):
http://www.LeisterPro.com

Palladium Interactive (Family Gathering):
    http://www.palladiumnet.com/palladium.html

Hamrick Software:
    http://www.hamrick.com/names/

Global Heritage Center:
    http://www.ledet.com/genealogy

Sausage Software (HotDog):
    http://www.sausage.com

PKWARE Inc. (WinZip):
    http://www.pkware.com/Welcome.html

Alladin Systems Inc. (StuffIt Expander):
    http://www.aladdinsys.com/consumer/expander1.html

General History

Index to History Network Resources:
    http://blair.library.rhodes.edu/histhtmls/histnet.html

Tennessee Tech History Web Site:
    http://www.tntech.edu/www/acad/hist/history.html

Heraldry

British Heraldry Archive:
    http://www.kwtelecom.com/heraldry/

International Heraldry:
    http://128.220.1.164/heraldry/intro.html

Armorial Heritage Foundation:
    http://www.hookup.net/~dbirk/chf.html

Heraldry on the Internet:
    http://digiserve.com/heraldry/

Photography

Buck's Photography Page:
    http://ourworld.compuserve.com/homepages/bills_fotos

Family Photo Shop:
    http://ourworld.compuserve.com/homepages/
    Family_Photo_Shop/

Williams Photo Restoration:
    http://www.prairienet.org/business/photo/photo.htm

Just Black & White:
    http://www.maine.com/photos/

Booksellers

Amazon.com Books:
    http://www.amazon.com/

Antiquarian Booksellers:
    http://www.abaa-booknet.com/

Zarahemla Book Shoppe:
    http://www.xmission.com/~zarahmla

Frontier Press:
    http://www.doit.com/frontier/frontier.cgi

Blair's Book Service:
    http://www.genealogy.com/blairs

Willow Bend Books:
    http://server.mediasoft.net/ScottC

Genealogical Publishing Company:
    http://www.genealogical.com/

Ancestry Search:
    http://www.ancestry.com/

Appleton's Books:
    http://www.moobasi.com

Internet Access/Web Space Providers

AT&T WorldNet
  http://www.att.com/worldnet/

Microsoft Network
  http://www.msn.com/

SPRYNET:
  http://www.sprynet.com/

America Online:
  http://www.aol.com/

CompuServe:
  http://www.compuserve.com/

Prodigy:
  http://www.prodigy.com/

WebTV:
  http://www.webtv.com/

Web Search Engines

AltaVista:
  http://www.altavista.digital.com/

WebCrawler:
  http://www.webcrawler.com/

Lycos:
  http://www.lycos.com/

Yahoo!
  http://www.yahoo.com/

Deja News:
  http://www.dejanews.com/

All in One:
  http://home.microsoft.com/access/allinone.asp

Miscellaneous

U.S. Presidents:
http://www.dcs.hull.ac.uk/public/genealogy/presidents/
gedx.html

Royal and Noble Genealogies:
http://www.dcs.hull.ac.uk/public/genealogy/GEDCOM.html

Mayflower Web Page:
http://members.aol.com/calebj/mayflower.html

HMS Bounty Genealogies:
http://wavefront.wavefront.com/~pjlareau/bounty6.html

Troubleshooting

Problems with Internet Access

My modem makes the usual whistling noises when I try to log in to my Internet service provider, but the noise continues, without any connection being made. Your modem is having trouble completing the "handshaking" with the modem at the other end of the connection. The most likely causes are (1) a noisy phone connection, or (2) an incorrect configuration (such as giving your software the wrong brand name or model of modem). Switch your modem off, then on again, and try re-dialing. If this doesn't help, double-check your software configuration. If the problem persists, contact your Internet service provider.

When I receive an incoming phone call when logged in to the Internet, my call waiting tone interferes with my session. In many areas local phone carriers provide a "tone block" option to customers which allows them to dial a prefix (*70 in the Washington, D.C., area, for example) that will temporarily suspend call waiting for the duration of a single phone call. If you have this feature, you should enter this prefix into your dial-up software as part of the number.

Problems with Web Browsing

My Web browser loads part of a document, then seems to get "hung." Although the Web browser may just be loading a large document, it is possible that a noisy line has caused a "glitch" that is interfering with the download. Try clicking on the STOP button and reloading the document. If you are running with a relatively small amount of memory (less than 16 megabytes), this may also indicate that you are running out of memory. You can adjust the "caching" options of your Web browser and close any other applications on your desktop that you don't need. If this doesn't help, exit the browser program and restart it.

Graphics images are being displayed in false color. This may indicate that your machine does not have enough memory to display the image in the proper number of colors. In this case a smaller set of colors (palette) is being used. Try freeing up memory as described above and, if necessary, restarting your browser program. You should also ensure that your windowing system has been configured to display at least 256 colors.

When I try to click on a hypertext link, my Web browser tells me that document loading is in progress. A Web browser cannot simultaneously load two documents. If it is still attempting to load a previous document, click on the STOP button before attempting to load another.

When I start my Web browser, it automatically dials up my Internet service provider, even though I only want to browse local documents. A Web browser will only invoke a dialer program if you are attempting to browse a document at a remote URL. If you use the configuration option of your Web browser to specify an HTML document which resides on your local machine, it will not automatically dial out when you start the program.

I am getting a "file not found" error. If you have typed in the URL manually, make sure there are no typos. If not, it may be that the document (or the entire Web site) has moved. One trick that is sometimes useful is to enter only a portion of the URL, lopping off the actual filename (but leaving a final forward slash, /). This will sometimes reveal other files that are present. It may be that a filename has been changed without all references to it being updated.

I am getting a message saying that an unexpected "end of file" has occurred. This is a problem with the HTML document, indicating that the writer inserted an HTML tag without its corresponding "closing" tag. If the document is on your local machine, add the missing tag. If not, it may be difficult to browse it. You can try downloading it to your local machine and making edits there.

A table of data on a Web page is coming up garbled. Some older Web browsers do not support the formatting of HTML tables. (Still older browsers do not support forms.) Since many Web pages today routinely use tables, it is a good idea to obtain a recent Web browser that supports them.

A Web search engine is not showing me a document that I know is out there and satisfies the search criteria. Web search engines only know about a Web page if someone adds the page to the engine's database. If you know of a useful page that is not turning up from a search, add it to the search engine's database yourself. This will assist others in your area of interest.

When I ask my Web browser to show the source (HTML tags) for the current document, it tells me that no source is available. Most likely, this is either because you are browsing an FTP-style hierarchy of directories and files (in which case there is no "document" as such), or because you have used the BACK button to display the screen. When you back up to a previous screen, some Web browsers retrieve the screen information from stored memory (a cache), without consulting the source again. If you reload the page, the source will again become available.

A document that I can browse on the Web can't be properly displayed after I download it to my local machine. This may be because of differing file naming conventions, or because the document makes use of CGI scripts. In order to execute a CGI script, a document must reside on a Web server. For example, an odometer-style counter showing the user's "visitor number" will not display properly if you download the document to your local machine.

I am getting a message saying that a host is not reachable (or my connection timed out). This could be caused by any of several things: (1) a typo in the URL, (2) the host machine referenced being down, or (3) if the machine is very far away, the intermediate nodes in the Internet may be having difficulty resolving the actual IP address. If you know the actual, numeric IP address, you can enter that in place of the mnemonic name. If not, you might want to try again later.

I am getting a message saying that too many anonymous FTP users are logged in to a host. To prevent system overloading, most anonymous FTP sites have a maximum number of simultaneous, anonymous logins that are allowed. Unless the site has alternate, "mirror" sites (other physical machines containing the same information), the only recourse is to wait a while and try again later.

My Web browser tells me that I can't send mail by clicking on a "mailto" URL. This is probably because you haven't set your e-mail address in the configuration of your Web browser. If you want to use your Web browser to send e-mail (which is what a "mailto" URL does), the browser needs to know what return address to put on the message. (This same e-mail information is used to automatically enter passwords for anonymous ftp logins.)

Problems with E-mail

A message I sent "bounced back" to me with a message saying that the mail was undeliverable. This could be the result of a typo in the e-mail address, or the recipient's mail server may be down. Since e-mail messages are seldom sent directly from the sender's to the recipient's computer, it may also be that an intermediate computer necessary for the proper routing of the message has gone down. If the address is correct, try again. If you get another bounce, try reaching the recipient some other way (by phone, for example) and verify that the address is correct.

When someone sends me an attached file, it appears at the end of the e-mail note in a strange encoded format. This probably indicates that the attached file is binary. Even though it is possible to attach a binary file to an e-mail message, all e-mail is actually sent in text format. You must use a decoding program such as uudecode or binhex to recover the original binary file.

When I send mail to someone who has a blank space as part of their e-mail address, my e-mail software won't allow the space. Some online services, such as America Online, allow the alternate use of underscore characters (_) in place of the blank.

My e-mail software is saying that another session is active, and won't let me log in to my mail server. It may be that a previous mail session was disconnected without your properly logging out (for example, you may have re-booted your local computer). Such "phantom" sessions usually time out after a period of inactivity. If you wait a while, you should have no trouble logging back in.

Sometimes e-mail notes I receive are broken into several separate notes. Why is this? This is done purely due to size constraints. Some e-mail packages (such as Eudora) allow you to manipulate a multi-part e-mail message as a single, logical entity.

Problems with Web Space

An ASCII file that looks fine on my local machine seems to be garbled after I upload to my Web server. This could be because there are two different conventions used to flag the end of a line of text (IBM PCs and compatibles use one method; everyone else uses the other). One way to correct this is to save the file in Unix format (some text editors allow this); another way is to use the "cr" command supported in some versions of FTP to remove extraneous carriage returns.

A graphics file does not seem to be valid after I upload it to the Web server. You may have transferred the file in ASCII mode; graphics files must be transferred in binary mode. Make sure that your FTP program is using binary mode and upload the file again.

When I browse the host version of my HTML document, my Web browser can't find a file, even though I know it's in the correct directory. Make sure that the syntax of the URLs in your host's Web document is compliant with its operating system (probably Unix). For example, if the version of your document down on your local machine uses drive specifiers (such as "C:\"), these must be removed from the host version. It is often helpful to use relative URLs (such as "./photos/gramps.jpg", indicating that the photo resides in the directory "photos," which is one level below the current directory—whatever that is). This way, the same HTML document can reside on two computers having differing file systems.

How can I make changes to the host version of my HTML document? It is best to keep the two versions of your Web document (the host version and the local version) "in sync" as much as possible. If you must change the host version, you probably need to use the emacs editor. There are also friendly public domain editors available for Unix, such as "pico." Ask your Web space provider what editors are available on your system.

Glossary

ahnentafel: A numbering system in which a focus individual is assigned the number 1; ancestors are assigned numbers which increase within each generation by visiting fraternal branches of the family tree first. (The sequence is: father, mother, father's father, father's mother, etc.)

anchor: The HTML tag used to define a hypertext link.

anonymous FTP: An account established on an Internet server which allows access to anyone on the Net; this access usually requires the user's full e-mail address as a password. (Web browsers usually provide this password automatically.)

ASCII: American Standard Code for Information Interchange. ASCII files are normally displayed as human-readable text files. These files can usually be exchanged between different computers, although sometimes the two differing conventions for flagging the end of a line of text may necessitate conversion. (Web browsers are able to recognize both types and usually make this distinction transparent to the user.)

baud: A number indicating the speed with which a modem can transfer data, expressed in bits per second. Many modem manufacturers are making the transition to the more modern term "kilobits per second" (kbps).

BBS: Bulletin Board System. A computer equipped with communications hardware and software enabling users to connect to it remotely by modem. Though many are still in use, BBSs are rapidly being replaced by servers on the Internet made possible by the newer TCP/IP protocol.

binary: Refers to electronically stored data intended to be read by computers, not human beings. Types of binary files include executable programs, compressed data, and graphics files. (Examples of these are files ending in .EXE, .ZIP, and .GIF, respectively.)

bit: Binary digit; this is the fundamental unit of information processed by computers. A bit can assume a value of 0 or 1.

byte: A grouping of eight bits. Software very seldom presents data for human perusal in fundamental units of bits, but rather groups it into these more convenient units. A character of text occupies one byte. Thus, a text file having a size of 2K (meaning two kilobytes) contains roughly two thousand characters.

case-sensitive: Distinguishing between uppercase and lowercase characters. Some operating systems, such as Unix, are case-sensitive. (For example, the Unix command "ls" will not be recognized if the user types in the uppercase "LS." DOS, on the other hand, will treat the input strings "dir" and "DIR" interchangeably.)

CGI script: Common Gateway Interface script. A computer program that can be invoked from an HTML document. The script produces outputs that are incorporated into the document being browsed. For example, an odometer-style counter showing the user's "visitor number" is the result of invoking a CGI script.

chat room (chat area): A feature offered by several popular online services in which users can chat in "real time" (as opposed to sending e-mail, which is stored on a mail server and opened later, as you would open a conventional letter).

client: A computer which is remotely accessing software or data on another system (the server). Your home computer is a client of the host machine you dial into when you connect to the Internet. Sometimes a program running on a client machine is also said to be a client.

data compression (as it applies to files): The technique of replacing a file with a smaller, or compressed, version which contains equivalent information, and from which the original file can be recovered. Large files are often compressed before transmittal across the Internet.

domain name: The final portion of an IP address, which follows the node name. Typically, the domain name includes the last two qualifiers of the IP address (such as "aol.com").

download: To copy a file from a host computer on the Internet onto your local computer.

editor (text editor): A software program designed to allow creation and modification of readable text files. Unlike word processors, text editors do not need to support special characters to indicate italics, boldface, or other document formatting.

E-mail: Electronic mail, typically sent across the Internet and stored on a mail server to be read later.

FAQ: Frequently Asked Question. Actually, a "FAQ" (pronounced "fak") is a list of frequently asked questions along with their answers. Such lists are valuable to newcomers. Users who are participating in a discussion group for the first time should locate and read the FAQ before posting questions.

form: A screen at which a user can type several inputs and submit them simultaneously to a host program. Web search engines use forms to gather keywords for which to search.

freeware: A software product which may be freely used and distributed, provided that no changes are made to the program. If the author further relinquishes copyright ownership, the program is said to be in the "public domain."

FTP: File Transfer Protocol. The protocol (and the associated software) used in the TCP/IP environment to transmit files between computers. A scheme of "ftp" in a URL allows Web browsers to fetch files without requiring the user to explicitly launch a separate FTP program.

GED2HTML: A utility written by Gene Stark which converts genealogical databases from the GEDCOM format into an HTML document.

GEDCOM: A standard file format designed by the Family History Department of The Church of Jesus Christ of Latter-day Saints. GEDCOM stands for GEnealogical Data COMmunication. GEDCOM files are used to transfer genealogical data between otherwise incompatible software packages or computers.

GIF: Graphic Interchange File. A type of graphics file which is widely used in HTML documents for inline images.

helper application: A program that is automatically started (launched) by a Web browser to display or process data that the browser could not otherwise handle.

host machine: A computer from which a user can retrieve data through an Internet connection; also, a server.

hotlist: A list of favorite URLs maintained by Web-browsing software which can be readily updated on the user's local machine. Also known as bookmark.

HTML: HyperText Markup Language. The language used to write documents which are browsed via the World Wide Web. Documents written in HTML may consist of hypertext as well as imbedded graphics.

HTTP: HyperText Transfer Protocol. The method by which the different components of documents are transferred across the World Wide Web. The HTTP specification prescribes the formats of requests and responses exchanged between clients and servers on the Web.

hypertext: Text in which highlighted key words (links) can be selected by a user to bring up a different document or a different passage within the same document

inline image: An image that is imbedded within an HTML document. Inline images are usually displayed automatically without the need for helper applications.

internal link: A hypertext link that takes the reader to another passage within the same document.

Internet: The global collection of computers, together with their associated communications links and support software, that make the computers accessible to anyone running TCP/IP software.

Internet Explorer: Microsoft's Web browser. Originally provided for Windows 95, but now also available for Windows 3.1.

Internet service provider (ISP): A company or organization that makes communications links to the Internet available to users. Some providers offer other services, such as e-mail, hobbyist, or special interest areas, and "chat" areas, as well as ftp or telnet accounts.

InterNIC: The NSFnet Network Information Center. This organization, among other things, is responsible for the registration of unique domain names for new users of the Internet.

IP address: Internet Protocol Address. The fully qualified name which uniquely specifies a node (computer) on the Internet. IP addresses are usually specified using mnemonic node and domain names (such as ftp.cac.psu.edu), but they may also be specified by their numeric equivalents (such as 129.119.19.103)

Java: A programming language used to instruct "Java-aware" Web browsers how to process the data requested by the user. Java is especially well suited to carry out intensive calculations on the user's local machine, such as real-time graphical animation.

JPEG: A graphics format devised by the Joint Photographic Experts Group. JPEG files are usually more compact than GIF files, and thus are better suited for the display of large or complex images.

link: A pointer (text or graphical) that leads the user to another document or a different passage within the same document.

Linux: A low-cost version of the Unix operating system.

listserver: A program which collects postings from users in a manner similar to that of a newsgroup, with the exception that postings are automatically sent via e-mail to subscribers to the list.

local machine: The computer at which a user is seated and is actually controlling (typically an IBM PC compatible or Macintosh); as opposed to a host machine (such as a Unix-based workstation operating as a Web server)

Lynx: A Web browser that is text-based. Useful for Web access from workstations (such as older, remote terminals) which do not have the ability to display graphics.

markup language: A language in which document formatting instructions (tags) are incorporated into human-readable text files; HTML is an example of a markup language.

mirror: To place the identical Web document at two locations so that twice as many people can access it at once. Some European pages are mirrored in the United States to make access easier for Americans. Mirrored documents have multiple URLs.

Mosaic: A Web browser; similar to *Netscape Navigator.* There are several versions of *Mosaic,* including both shareware and commercial products.

name server: A computer which is consulted by TCP/IP-based software (such as Web browsers) to convert, or "resolve," mnemonic IP addresses into their numeric equivalents.

Net: A shortened form of "Internet."

Netscape: Netscape Communications Corporation. The developers of the widely used *Netscape Navigator* Web browser. Many people abbreviate the phrase "Netscape Navigator" to "Netscape."

Netscape Navigator: The most widely-used Web browser; other similar products are *Mosaic* and Microsoft's *Internet Explorer.*

newsgroup: A repository to which users can post questions, responses, or announcements relating to a specific area of interest.

newsreader: A software program which displays lists of the newsgroups available on your news server and which lets you browse and post messages to groups of your choice.

node: A computer connected to the Internet; a node is connected to a domain. The node *name* is usually the first part of the URL following "http://" (or other scheme).

online: Connected to the Internet, or more generally, connected to one or more computers through any communications link. A person who is "online" has access to the Internet.

operating system: The software programs which must be running on any computer before it can accept user requests or execute any of the user's "application" software (word processors, spreadsheets, etc.) Examples of operating systems are DOS, Windows 95, Unix, System 7.

POP: Post Office Protocol. A method of transferring accumulated mail residing on a mail server to a local machine. This is done automatically when you check your mail if you are running TCP/IP software on your local machine.

posting: A message which is appended to a newsgroup or list server to be read by others interested in the same subject area.

PPP: Point-to-Point Protocol. A protocol by which a computer which is not directly connected to a network can communicate through a modem. If you run TCP/IP software on your local machine, that software is probably using PPP to communicate with your Internet access provider.

public domain: Available freely to the general public. Public domain software can be used free of charge so long as it is not modified and passed on to others.

scheme: The first part of a URL, such as "http," "ftp," or "gopher."

search engine: Software residing on a Web server which allows a user to search documents on the Web for specified keywords.

server: A computer which is retrieving data or running programs at the request of a remote computer (the client). Also called a host.

shareware: Software which is made available on a trial basis. If a user chooses to use the product regularly, it is understood that he/she will send an amount of money requested by the author or distributor.

snail mail: Conventional, paper mail. The term is often used to distinguish it from e-mail, with an emphasis on the differing lengths of time required for delivery.

socket: The connection between the TCP/IP software on your local machine and the Internet.

tag: A command in a markup language (such as HTML) that instructs a software product (such as a Web browser) to format the selected text in a specified way.

TCP/IP: Transmission Control Protocol/Internet Protocol. The combination of protocols used for communications across the Internet.

telnet: A protocol used in the TCP/IP environment to allow remote login to a host machine. The term also refers to the program used to initiate a telnet session, and is also used as a verb: *to telnet to a remote host.*

thread: A sequence of newsgroup postings which are all on the same topic. Some newsreader programs arrange postings by thread, making it easier to identify at a glance postings which are of interest.

tiny tafel: A compact text format in which the contents of a family database can be summarized and readily provided to other researchers. Unlike GEDCOM, the tiny tafel (TT) format is not intended to encapsulate all genealogical information in a database, but rather to advertise what information is available.

Unix: A very powerful, multi-user, multi-tasking operating system which is especially well-equipped for telecommunications. For this reason, many Web servers run Unix.

upload: To transfer a file from a local computer to a remote host; usually done by means of FTP

URL: Uniform Resource Locator. A string of characters that identifies a document or location within a document on the World Wide Web that is to be browsed. These are the "addresses" that you can either click on or type into a Web browser that take you to a desired Web page.

Web authoring tool: An editor program that provides easy point-and- click options to create or edit HTML tags. Such a tool speeds up the process of writing an HTML document by eliminating redundant text entry. It also makes it unnecessary to learn complex HTML tags.

Web browser: A program, such as *Netscape Navigator* or *Mosaic,* which allows the user to view documents written in HTML.

Web page: A document which is accessed via the World Wide Web. If a Web page is an author's main page, from which all other pages are accessed, it is called a *home page.*

Web space provider: A company or organization that rents or otherwise makes available disk space on its Web server on which an author may store his or her HTML documents. By placing their documents on such a server, authors make them accessible to anyone having access to the World Wide Web.

World Wide Web (WWW or Web): That portion of the Internet that communicates by means of HyperText Transfer Protocol (HTTP). Documents on the World Wide Web are written in the HyperText Markup Language (HTML) and are viewed with a Web browser.

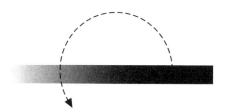

Index

G

Gaunt, Chris, 41
GED2HTML
   conversion to HTML by, 85
   created by, 85
   example of, 91-92
   See also HyperText Markup
     Language (HTML)
GEDCOM
   as common language, 56
   complexity of, 59
   as data base files, 22, 33, 57-59
   developed by, 56
   export versus import of, 57-58
   output control and, 71-73
   purpose of, 57
   as standard text format, 56-57
   trends for, 59
   versus HTML, 58, 59, 85
   Web and, 58
   See also Internet service
    providers (ISP)
Genealogical supplies, online
   resources for, 64
Genealogy Gateway, 51, 118
Genealogy Home Page, 50, 117
Genealogy (numbering systems)
   ancestors system of, 78-79
   descendant system of, 76-77
   software use of, 76
   See also Ahnentafel system;
    Register numbering system
Genealogy online
   accuracy of data of, 55
   bookstore locations for, 62-64
   census data, 52-53
   home pages for, 50-51, 117-131
   local resources and, 61-64
   pedigrees, 54-56
   regional history, 60-61
   search engines for, 59
   social security data, 52-53
   vital statistics and, 51-52, 54
   See also Web site locations;
   Regional histories; Home page
   creation; Web browsers; Internet
   service providers (ISP)

Genealogy societies, online
   resources for, 126-127
Genealogy (software)
   data decompression in, 78-81
   data organization in, 67
   data sharing, 67
   data storage of, 73
   electronic photographs and, 70
   generation of trees in, 67
   output control of, 71-73
   record identification numbers
    in, 70-71
   search capability of, 73
   shareware, 66-67
   Web location of, 73-74
   See also Web site locations
General history, online resources
   for, 128
GenServ
   browser versus down loading
    on, 59
   as genealogical database, 59
Geocities, 103, 104
Gore, Al (Senator), 11
Graphics
   commands for, 52
   download time of, 99
   file format of, 98-99
   file formats, 98
   gray scale versus color for, 97
   HTML embedded codes for, 97
   quantity of, 99
   resolution level of, 97-98
   small versus big in, 99
   See also Home page creation;
    Publishing home pages
Gray scale image, 97
Gunn, Mike, 52

H

Harvard University, 8
Helm's Genealogy Toolbox, 50, 60,
   61, 117
Heraldry, online resources for, 128
Hickman, Deborah, 60
High Performance Computer
   (Act), 11

You never know who you'll meet at Ancestry HomeTown...

Like your great-great grandmother. Or maybe a distant cousin you never knew you had. Or perhaps a genealogy expert who can help you with the long-lost ancestor you've been tracking for years.

Ancestry HomeTown is the largest and most diverse online genealogical community anywhere in the world. More than twenty thousand people visit our Web site each day, and chances are some of them can help you find what you're looking for. And with a subscription to Ancestry HomeTown's vast library of genealogical databases—featuring a new database added every day—you'll be able to tap into the largest source of genealogy records, reference books, and biographical and historical information on the World Wide Web.

Stop by http://www.ancestry.com today and take a look at everything Ancestry HomeTown has to offer. Then subscribe to Ancestry's complete database library for the low monthly price of $4.95. Whether you're new to the fascinating world of genealogy, or a family history expert with thousands of names in your database, you'll find that Ancestry HomeTown will help make genealogy easier, more fun, and more rewarding than ever before. And maybe you'll run into someone you didn't expect—like that elusive great-great grandma of yours.

- **The largest genealogical community on the World Wide Web**

- **A new database added every day**

- **The latest news and columns from the experts in the world of genealogy**

- **Free Community GEDCOM Tree**

- **Great deals on genealogy products**

- **Online tutorials and classes for both beginners and experts**

Ancestry HomeTown: http://www.ancestry.com